D1431025

Ex libris
Beth-el Hebrew Congregation
NORTHERN VIRGINIA

THE
STATE PAPERS
OF
LEVI ESHKOL

LEVI ESHKOL

1895–1969

THE STATE PAPERS OF LEVI ESHKOL

EDITED, WITH AN INTRODUCTION, BY

Henry M. Christman

Funk & Wagnalls

NEW YORK

Library of Congress Catalog Card Number: 69–19650
Published by Funk & Wagnalls,
A Division of Reader's Digest Books, Inc.

Printed in the United States of America

Contents

Introduction

OF ALL THE strife-torn areas of the world, none approaches the Middle East in ultimate significance for world peace. How ironic that this historic region, the cradle of Western civilization, could become the cause and origin of a world war that would destroy that same Western civilization.

It is, therefore, imperative that the basic issues affecting the stability of the Middle East be understood by the widest possible public. To this end, the following book brings together for the first time the authoritative statements of the State of Israel as set forth by Prime Minister Levi Eshkol.

Of course, much has been said and written about the Middle East in general and Israel in particular.

This book, however, is unique, because it constitutes the authoritative documents of the State of Israel, the official positions of the Government of Israel.

Depending upon the reader's interest and approach in the subject, this book can serve him in any one of three ways.

For those interested in a panoramic view of the issues and challenges facing Israel as it enters its third decade, this book presents the policy of the Government of Israel on the major questions of national and international affairs.

For those interested in the historic Six-Day War, a military and political event second in importance only to Israel's War of Independence, this book contains the state documents tracing the day-by-day and even hour-by-hour developments leading up to the war, and a graphic chronology of the war itself.

Finally, for those interested in a profile of the leader of Israel during this crucial and historic period, the personality and concerns of Levi Eshkol the man emerge as he guides the Government toward its national and international goals.

Israel's amazing and inspiring success is all the more impressive when consideration is given to the obstacles.

There is the physical problem of the land itself, the necessity for quickly reclaiming and developing a largely arid region with few raw materials and few natural resources.

There is the economic problem, that of developing Israel as a balanced, self-sufficient industrial economy able to give full and productive employment to her citizens.

There is the human problem not only of training and utilizing native Israelis to their fullest potential, but also the challenge of quickly absorbing destitute immigrants of many cultures and backgrounds, without modern skills, and transforming them into productive workers and, moreover, into responsible citizens ready to play their full role in Israel's dynamic democracy.

There is the human problem of the non-Jewish Israeli citizens, that of helping them to develop their own fullest potential in their own way, retaining their distinctive cultures and languages, and yet bringing them directly into the mainstream of Israeli democracy and political life.

There is the further human problem of the Arab non-citizens in the territories administered by Israel as a result of the Six-Day War, whose ultimate fate is undetermined.

And, finally, there is the overriding problem of the continued hostility of neighboring Arab nations, which affects every aspect of life and planning in Israel. It is no exaggeration to say that this is one of the tragedies of modern history. Israel, which has so much to offer her neighbors in the way of modern technological expertise, is rejected by them and must divert much-needed funds and manpower from economic development to military defense.

Each of these problems is complex. Each is imperative. All are interrelated, and all must be solved. And they must be solved democratically, for it must never be forgotten that Israel is one of the most lively and truly dynamic democracies in the world, with a broad spectrum of political viewpoints, zealous protection of civil rights and civil liberties, and an outspoken free press. Israel, as a state and as a society, is dedicated to the freedom and fulfillment of the human spirit.

Such is the challenge facing Israel and her Prime Minister, Levi Eshkol. For more than half a century, his life has been intimately associated with the achievement of the Zionist ideal, the rebirth of Israel as a modern state.

Levi Eshkol was born in 1895 in Orotavo, a railway junction in the "Jewish Pale" section of the Ukraine, one of the restricted areas in which Czarist Russia permitted Jews to settle. The family name was Shkolnik, which he Hebraised to Eshkol (meaning "cluster of grapes") after Israel achieved independence. Young Eshkol's family was well-to-do; his mother, Dvora Krasnunsky, came from a wealthy, influential family, while his father, Joseph, was both a businessman and a dedicated member of the Hasidim. Young Eshkol and his nine brothers and one sister were tutored at home by young Hebrew scholars, and later Eshkol attended the Hebrew Gymnasium in Vilna, Poland.

In 1914, at the age of nineteen, Eshkol emigrated to Palestine. When he arrived at what is now Tel Aviv—today a bustling, cosmopolitan city—it was then only a small village. Within two days after his arrival in Palestine, Eshkol was working as an agricultural laborer, reclaiming land at Petach Tikva. He later became a founding member of Degania Beth, a Jordan Valley kibbutz.

Following the close of World War I, the Jewish

agricultural workers in Palestine organized a union, setting up labor exchanges, health insurance and welfare funds, and educational programs. Eshkol was active in this movement, and was elected as a member of the Central Council. Out of these activities grew Histadrut, the General Federation of Labor, formally organized in 1921. Eshkol was asked to direct Histadrut's farming activities, his first responsibility as a Histadrut executive. For the next two decades, Eshkol played a major part in Histadrut's development, establishing and promoting new Histadrut corporations for investment, water supply and irrigation, contracting and housing. During this period, he also directed the Jewish Agency's program to rescue Jewish refugees from Germany and to transfer Jewish property to Palestine.

In 1944, Eshkol became Secretary-General of the Tel Aviv Labor Council, the largest body of organized labor in Palestine. During the 1940s, he also played a major role in the organization of the Haganah, the underground volunteer army. Eshkol served as treasurer of Haganah, and developed its secret military industries division, which produced arms vital to the independence movement. Upon the declaration of statehood in 1948, Eshkol became Director-General of the Ministry of Defense in the new government.

In less than a year following independence, Israel faced an economic crisis. The new state welcomed Jewish refugees from abroad, but the sudden influx of hundreds of thousands of penniless immigrants critically strained the food and housing resources of the nation. The problems were manifold. In order to feed the greatly expanded population, food production had to be increased rapidly, which, in turn, required not only greater agricultural efficiency on existing farms, but also the early reclamation of vast barren areas. The human problems were even more complex; hundreds of thousands of newcomers from all over the world had to be integrated into Israeli society. And time was of the essence; both economic necessity and the hostility of surrounding Arab nations demanded that the immigrants be integrated as quickly as possible.

Levi Eshkol's background in agriculture, labor, and economic planning made him uniquely qualified to meet this critical situation. He took charge as director of the Land Settlement Department of the Jewish Agency, and was instrumental in founding almost 500 new villages throughout Israel. Under Eshkol's humane guidance, immigrants were not detained in refugee camps, but instead were placed directly on farms and villages. The challenge was met; due to Eshkol, Israel's food production was rapidly increased, key new settlements were established to strengthen Israeli population distribution throughout the nation, and the refugees rapidly became skilled, valuable workers and proud, integral members of Israel's new society.

In 1951, Eshkol entered the Cabinet as Minister of Agriculture. In 1952, he became Minister of Finance, a post he was to hold for twelve years. When David Ben-Gurion retired in 1963 as Prime Minister and as head of Mapai, the Israel Labor Party, Eshkol succeeded him in both posts, and also assumed the Cabinet post of Minister of Defense. In 1967, Eshkol broadened the Cabinet non-politically in response to the crisis of the Six-Day War, relinquishing the Defense Ministry but retaining the post of Prime Minister.

In his six years as Prime Minister, Levi Eshkol has dealt with problems ranging from scientific research on desalination of seawater to the reunification of historic Jerusalem to the question of diplomatic relations between Israel and the Federal Republic of Germany. All these concerns are reflected in the documents gathered together for the first time in this book. Here is the official, definitive Government position on the national and international issues facing Israel. Through Premier Eshkol, Israel speaks to its citizens and to the world.

As editor, I, of course, bear sole responsibility for the book, for the selections herein, and for the initiation of this publishing endeavor.

Levi Eshkol, 1895–1969

On February 26, 1969, only a few hours before this book—which had been more than a year in preparation—was to go to press, the world was stunned and saddened by the sudden and untimely death of Prime Minister Eshkol.

This book serves to present and perpetuate his ideas and ideals, his goals and accomplishments.

Levi Eshkol was a pioneer Zionist who served the cause of Israel with total dedication for more than half a century. He was a remarkable man of many talents who brought to his chosen life-work a rare combination of idealism, activism, and judiciousness.

His ultimate vision went far beyond the immediate problems of the State of Israel; he intensely desired permanent regional and world peace that would permit Israel to devote her full resources to what he passionately believed to be her destiny, that of the further development of a model society that would inspire and assist unparalleled progress among all the peoples of the Middle East and the world.

Israel's Levi Eshkol was, therefore, a world statesman in the fullest sense of the term—a humanitarian whose life, thought, and policies were founded upon great ideals that are both universal and timeless. It is my hope that this book will serve to further his ideals.

HENRY M. CHRISTMAN

Independence Day Address

April 15, 1964

On the eve of the 17th year of Israel's independence I bring the greetings of the Government to all Israel at home and throughout the Diaspora. May this be a year of immigration, security, and consolidation.

On this day it is our hope that all Jews at home and abroad will intensify their devotion to the common national aims of the consolidation and progress of Israel, and the enhancement of the Jewish content of life in the Diaspora.

During the past year we were once again privileged to welcome large numbers of immigrants. Our capacity to bring them in and to absorb them has again been tested, and we have stood the test. The past year's immigration brings us still nearer to the stage when we shall have completed the task of bringing in those Jews from the lands of distress who are free to settle in Israel. We note this with both satisfaction and concern: satisfaction at our achievements and concern for the future.

On this day we cherish the hope for the opening of the gates and the renewal of our contacts with those Jewish communities—especially a certain and important one—who are still cut off from the life of our people and from participation in our great task of redemption.

On this day, too, we look towards the lands of prosperity and call upon the Jewish communities to make their contribution—both material and human—to the consolidation of the State and the raising of its standards. We shall make every effort to help them to reawaken the Jewish spark in their lives and to walk in the light of Jewish ideals.

In summing up the work of the past year and sketching out lines of progress for the future, I shall start with the problem of security. I have no intention of laying down any scale of priorities, but it is obvious that unless Israel's physical survival is secured, we shall be unable to make progress in other spheres.

We have had a comparatively quiet year on the borders, but—to my regret—there has been no let-up in the threats of war from our neighbors; they have not made up their minds to acquiesce in Israel's existence as the foundation for a peace settlement.

Our enemies openly proclaim that war with Israel is inevitable at a date which they themselves will determine. We cannot ignore these threats; they compel us to maintain continual readiness, both for the days immediately ahead and for the more distant future when our neighbors will come to the conclusion that they have become strong enough to make a fresh attempt to carry out their designs. We must be prepared, with arms of sufficient quality and quantity, and with well-trained manpower and a strong economy, to repulse our enemies and to break the forces they are preparing against us. We must maintain the deterrent strength of the Israel Defense Forces, so that no one should cherish the thought that it is possible to challenge Israel to war.

During the past year we have increased our strength by improving the skills of our army, by putting into operation additional weapons, and by expanding our own arms manufacture. This progress will be partially reflected tomorrow at the Defense Forces' parade in Beersheba. We must continue to enhance our strength in all these and other spheres in the coming year, for it is a matter of life or death.

It gives me profound satisfaction today to send from here a special greeting to the Israel Defense Forces and to all the staffs of our defense establishment. Our lives—the survival of the State, the future of the Jewish people—are in your faithful hands. You are doing your work with great devotion, despite many difficulties and sometimes in complete anonymity. Be strong and of good courage.

In our foreign relations our policy is founded on the same concern for the preservation of our security despite the designs of our enemies. We shall persevere in our efforts to establish relations of friendship and peace. We do not accept the crude belief that the Arab-Jewish conflict is the dividing line between all the nations in the Middle East. The vital distinction is that between peace-loving nations and aggressors. While we must be ready to meet the dangers of aggression, we must seek out every factor—without distinction of nation or tongue—that is ready to contribute towards peace and stability in the Middle East, and offer our hand in peace and friendship.

Over the heads of our recalcitrant neighbors we shall continue to offer our friendship to the developing nations, most of which have recently been liberated from foreign tutelage. We can meet them as a nation that—like them—has regained its freedom in recent years, and share with them the fruits of the experience we have gained in rebuilding our country —in science, technology, and social values.

The great powers have an important part to play in ensuring stability and peace in the Middle East. There was a time, not so long ago, when we regarded the very recognition of Israel's existence as an achievement in itself. Now we call upon the great powers to help all the nations of the area to develop their economies, to improve social standards, and to achieve stability and peace. What is wanted is true development, which will bring prosperity to the masses and make it impossible to incite them against other nations. Let the great powers compete in such assistance and not in the supply of arms to potential aggressors, which compels us to devote to defense too large a part of the resources that should be dedicated to constructive development, and which obliges us to seek and demand the defense armaments that we require.

In full responsibility and goodwill, we have accepted the proposal that the use of force be ruled out as a method of settling international disputes. We are entitled to expect that the initiators of this proposal, and other powers as well, should make it perfectly clear to our neighbors that this principle applies to all, without exception. No country can be allowed to pretend to be a lover of peace by adopting a positive attitude towards disputes that are none of its concern, while continuing to utter threats of war against its neighbors.

At the present moment our enemies have not even accepted the principle of coexistence as a nominal obligation. Their threats of violence continue. We shall welcome any clear statement by friendly powers that no one will be allowed to commit aggression against us. But we cannot base our security on words alone, nor can we agree that our very existence should be dependent on the goodwill of others. As in all the other fields of endeavor—in economy, social life and culture—we must continue to rely first and foremost on ourselves, and enhance our own strength.

We are sincerely grateful for all the help we have had in building our economy and in integrating the immigrants; we have done our best to put it to good use. Humanity now stands on the threshold of an era in which the waters of the sea will be purified and used for the benefit of mankind. The water problem is becoming more and more urgent in many parts of the world; in our area it is already so. We hope to play our modest part in this effort to develop methods of desalinating sea water for the benefit of our own country, the entire Middle East, and the world at large. We should appreciate any assistance, both in know-how and in financial resources, in this effort.

We are entering into the practical stage in our relations with the European Common Market. This is only a small beginning; we are still far from obtaining what we require. It is our duty to make every possible effort to expand our export opportunities and to improve our trade relations, so that we may make progress towards economic independence, which alone will give full meaning to our political independence and give us the self-respect of a nation living on its own labors.

This is not a task for one year alone; all we can do is to point out the goal and mark out the direction. By the end of this decade we must reduce the gap between our imports and exports and make substantial progress towards the closing of it in the coming years. This calls for a tremendous effort to improve productivity and quality, and we shall have to impose a strict order of priorities in satisfying economic demands.

Our economic development is closely interwoven with our scale of social values. Our society cannot endure if it is founded on a collective and individual scale of values based on the benefits we draw from society and not on our contribution to society. Such a topsy-turvy scale of values leads to constant demands on the State even from circles which are not particularly backward or underprivileged, at times resulting in grave injury to the general welfare. The deplorable way of life, characterized by conspicuous consumption, of a few who pursue wealth, luxury, and comfort, should not be a will o' the wisp that beckons us to demand more and more.

All spheres of our activity, all our central aims, depend to no little extent on the character of the society we are building and on our capacity to unite on the basis of social and national values.

In order to restore respect for these values, we need the right kind of education. We must expand our education of all kinds in the spheres of knowledge and know-how; we have achieved much in this field, but not yet enough. But we cannot impart knowledge without at the same time imparting values; we cannot acquire prosperity if we turn our backs on the things of the spirit. Let us not deceive ourselves: voluntary effort, the readiness to take the lead and set an example—in one phrase, personal halutziut or pioneering, arising out of a free decision—will still be necessary for many years to come.

The State must prepare itself for a prolonged collective pioneering effort; it must create the frameworks, secure and supply the resources, give the lead, encourage, spur, and stimulate. For all these purposes it needs the contribution of the pioneer, who identifies himself utterly with the difficult historic tasks that we have undertaken.

A happy Independence Day to you all.

Statement at the First Meeting of the Joint United States-Israel Technical Team on the Desalting of Water

July 27, 1964

MR. AMBASSADOR, GENTLEMEN:

I am very glad to welcome you here and to open the meetings of the joint US-Israel technical team on the desalting of water.

I think there is no place in the world where as much attention is focussed on the subject of water as it is in Israel, and this is true not only of modern Israel but applies also to the ancient land of the Bible. In this part of the world civilization grew around water, and if we read our Bible carefully we can see that ancient Israelis were as "water conscious" as their modern successors.

Israel is not blessed with plentiful water resources: the big rivers of the fertile crescent all flow outside our territory; our real river, the Jordan, has a great name and a glorious history, but very little water. In ancient times, therefore, this has never been an irrigation country like its more fortunate neighbors—Egypt, Mesopotamia, and Syria.

The country that our new settlers found had very little resemblance to "a land flowing with milk and honey": most of it was dry—either dry-farming or desert, while in the north, where most of the natural water resources are concentrated, the country was swampy and malaria-ridden. Under such conditions, one indeed needs modern engineering to create irrigated agriculture. Since the establishment of the State of Israel in 1948, we have expanded irrigation from 75,000 to almost 400,000 acres.

Piped water supplies have been provided to every town and village, while the population grew from 850,000 to 2,500,000; all swamps have been drained and a modern industrial economy brought into being. This was done by mobilizing most of the water resources of the country; today, after the completion of the Jordan project, the country's largest water development undertaking, almost 85 per cent of the potential water resources are in use.

The remaining water resources will be fully utilized in the near future. We must therefore now look for ways and means to conserve our existing water resources, to increase the efficiency in their use, and to add to our natural water resources new man-made ones.

The rate of Israel's economic growth is today among the highest in the world; our economy will in all likelihood continue to grow rapidly in the future, and water will, of course, be a prerequisite of such further growth.

It is abundantly clear that additional water in Israel of the early seventies can mean only converted sea water: desalting is therefore an integral part of Israel's economic plans for the future. Five years ago, a high-level permanent commission was nominated to advise the Government of Israel on current action to be taken in connection with desalting. Three demonstration plants were initiated: one, based on the principle of freezing, is already operating at Eilat; the second, also at Eilat, based on flash evaporation, is now under construction and scheduled to start operating in the coming spring; the third, utilizing the principle of electrodialysis, will also be operating soon. All these plants, however, are not more than demonstration plants: what is now required are large-scale and highly efficient plants to convert sea water in large quantities. This is to us a vital necessity if we are to support the country's economic growth in the next decade. We fully realize that before we can meet this objective, a great deal of development and engineering work will be required.

Since the subsequent fabrication, erection and running-in of the necessary plant must consume considerable time, we in Israel feel that there is no time to lose. All necessary action must be taken now to initiate large-scale desalting and to proceed in a planned and coordinated way, in order to have the water available when we shall need it.

This was the background on which the offer made by President Johnson at the Weizmann Institute dinner for US-Israeli cooperation in the field of desalting sea water was received. It was with these needs in mind that I discussed this subject, on behalf of the Government of Israel, with the President.

Aware of the country's vital needs, the Israeli public takes intense interest in the work of the joint

US-Israeli study team which is now to commence.

Several circumstances and coincidences augur well for the US-Israeli cooperation put into stride by your group:

1) the decision of the government of the USA to develop desalting for the benefit of the arid regions of the world;

2) the existence of a vital need in Israel for desalting in the near future;

3) the existence in Israel of a type of economy that, I hope, justifies under certain conditions, the large-scale use of converted sea water both for non-agricultural and also for agricultural purposes;

4) the existence in Israel of large quantities of slightly saline water which can be improved by dilution with desalted sea water;

5) the existence in Israel of a sufficient number of engineers and scientists to support such development in cooperation with US engineers and scientists and

6) last but not least, the warm friendship that exists between the US and Israel ever since the establishment of the State of Israel—a friendship which found one of its most significant expressions in the recent joint US-Israel declaration on cooperation in the development of desalting.

I hope that the work of this joint US-Israeli team will result in determining adequate ways and means of large-scale desalting, so badly needed by Israel; that you will define an agreed line of action to be adopted in all phases of the proposed project, so as to arrive within a reasonable time at the desired result; and, that you will be able to make joint recommendations on the immediate steps to be taken upon the conclusion of the present first step in this US-Israeli great and, I would say, revolutionary joint venture.

I would like to emphasize that it was agreed between President Johnson and myself that the knowledge and experience obtained from this joint program will be made available to all countries with water deficiencies.

President Johnson is vigorously pursuing his great and imaginative idea of international cooperation in this vital field of using sea water for life and development. He has now called for an international conference to advance the process of research and cooperation in this area.

Israel is privileged indeed to have been included in this historic enterprise.

Gentlemen:

I wish you good progress in your forthcoming work, and look with anticipation to receiving your conclusions and recommendations in a few weeks' time.

Statement in the Knesset Concerning the Social Situation in Israel

---

December 8, 1964

THE JEWISH COMMUNITY in this country numbered a little more than 600,000 at the establishment of the State. Since then we have absorbed approximately double this number of immigrants from all the continents, speaking scores of languages, nurtured in various cultures, on all kinds of levels of development. Even today, of those who can read and write, only about 80% read and write Hebrew. A still smaller percentage know and speak Hebrew as their only or first language. The cultural gap stretches from illiteracy up to our finest men of science and culture . . .

We started to mould the character of the nation and build a state by a leap over intervening stages. We have repeatedly had to transfer groups of individuals and families not only from place to place but actually from era to era, from culture to culture, from regime to regime.

There is no single act that embodies this process. The links are closely interconnected: education, housing, development, agricultural settlement, way of life, social and political integration—all these dictate its speed. We cannot expect an overall solution by means of a break-through in one area alone . . .

The transfer of masses of Jews has not been merely an effort of transportation, but an effort of transplantation, with all the complicated care that this implies for all the parts of the plant, its roots and its branches. Complete communities, tribes, clans and families have been uprooted, and we have replanted them in the homeland . . . Remnants of Jewish communities in the world have brought with them cultural values in the broadest sense of the term: a complex of relationship between man and man and between man and community . . .

The majority of the immigrants went to establish new towns and fill up the old ones . . . Employment is one of the principal ladders for the social advancement of the immigrants . . . Only seven years ago, almost one third of the workers in the development towns were employed on relief works; three years ago less than 5% ; today the proportion can hardly be measured in percentages.

There has been a parallel transition from unskilled to skilled labor, from temporary to permanent employment. Many of the untrained workers of a few years ago are today foremen. To every industrial worker in the country up to the establishment of the State two new immigrants have been added.

About half the 50,000 members of workers' and staff committees are new immigrants, and a considerable proportion come from Asian and African countries. Particularly in the development towns, the new immigrants are bearing a growing share of the responsibility in the local trade union bodies.

Of course, there is still much to be done in these spheres. From the start, new immigrants naturally enter into less remunerative classes of employment and into the lower levels of these classes . . . Nevertheless, we may note progress in employment and a gradual rise in economic standards.

In immigrant areas, from north to south, we can already see the beginnings of a true organic growth of a local leadership elite, whose roots are in the local soil but whose vision, nevertheless, is not restricted to the limits of locality or community . . . Some of them have served in the army and risen to NCO's or officer's rank, and some have made progress in teaching or trade union activity . . .

When a man of this kind becomes head of a local council, he really belongs to the place . . . His first struggles are intimately connected with the place where he lives, and not with the swamps of decades ago . . . When such a man represents his community, he has no problems in finding a bridge to those who arrived before him.

Such a natural growth of a leadership elite automatically rectifies the communal balance . . . Thus the immigrants become integrated in the chain of pioneers who built the country since the beginnings of the Zionist settlement movement: a chain of immigration which absorbs further immigration.

The cope-stone of the new immigration's achievement is the new agricultural settlement, which is mainly a settlement of immigrants. The personal contribution that has been made and is being made to the maintenance of the State by men, women and children most of whom came here without physical or spiritual training, without years of preparation by an organized political movement and a conscious pioneering ideology, is inestimable . . .

They have learned to love this country, to cherish and defend its soil . . . They have adopted, through a great effort, our social and co-operative patterns in all their forms, and especially in the form of the moshav, the smallholders' co-operative settlement. The members of the immigrants' moshavim regard themselves—and act—like members of veteran settlements in all respects.

(Mr. Eshkol proceeded to give an example of the change in the attitude of one particular settler from Persia, who arrived almost illiterate twelve years ago and is now the owner of a model farm, and—even more notably—the change in the life of his son.)

It is this integration in the economic and social structure, by adopting its forms and values, that is characteristic of the process of social integration and the merging of the communities, not the generalized lamentations that are rife about the so-called abandonment of values. The opposite is the case: the overwhelming majority of two-thirds of our population brought no pioneering values with them from their parents' homes; they had nothing to abandon; they only had something to acquire. They have honorably stood the test in the crucibles of our society: in agricultural settlement, in the schools, and in the army.

The significance of integration in these settlements, with their communal concentrations, does not lie in the abolition of differences or the abandonment of values brought from the countries of origin, but their improvement and refinement, the raising of standards and the adoption of our common values . . .

There is no need to be an expert in problems of absorption and integration to perceive immediately the central role of education in this process, and it is particularly in this field that it is difficult to overleap the intervening stages. It is possible to speed up the construction of a house; it is impossible to speed up the growth of a child.

And the question is even more complex, because it is doubtful whether it can be solved in one generation . . . The child's capacity to study and absorb depends on the atmosphere of understanding in the home, and even on physical limitations, such as housing conditions . . . Tremendous efforts are being made, and growingly greater efforts will be required the more the country's demands for education grow.

Since the rise of the State, the number of pupils has grown *twice as much as the growth of the population;* free compulsory education has been fully implemented by law: half the three- and four-year-olds in need of it receive kindergarten education free —the number grows year by year and in two or three years will cover all those in need; post-primary education has been expanded, especially vocational education for industry, seafaring and agriculture; tuition fees are gradually ceasing to be a hindrance to the continuance of the child's education.

The development of all stages of education, the

special care given to certain groups, the comprehensive school which facilitates transfer from one subject to another, special care for the talented, the development of vocational education and its adaptation to the needs of a highly developed economy, the fivefold expansion of higher education since the rise of the State—all these are a part of the effort to reduce the gap between social strata . . .

Among the children of immigrants from African and Asian countries, almost 20,000 are already in kindergartens for three- and four-year-olds; they make up 60% of the children in kindergartens for five-year-olds; 43% in the primary schools; 20% in morning and evening secondary schools; 35% in vocational schools; 39% in agricultural schools; 14% in the continuation (secondary-standard) schools of the labor settlements; 25% in teachers' training colleges; 12% in institutes of higher learning.

We cannot say that this is enough, but it is a great deal: children of immigrants from Asia and Africa already make up about a quarter of the students in post-primary schools—over 22,000 . . .

We are not resting on our laurels. During the next five years we aim to double the number of children in the kindergartens. Free compulsory education will be extended by at least a year. Some 40,000 more children will join the post-primary schools, with vocational education being doubled. And that is not yet the end of the process.

To this we must add cultural activities among adults, and especially the comprehensive effort to extirpate illiteracy, which has covered some 10,000 students so far. Let me pay tribute to the assistance of service-women in these efforts: it may be said that an entire regiment of service-women has come forward to help our educational work.

I cannot refrain from recalling the voluntary efforts of individuals and groups who have renewed the tradition of "going to the people."

(Mr. Eshkol recalled the work of Jewish young men and women among the Russian peasants in past generations and continued:) Is it too much to expect of our youth and intelligentsia to come forward for such an effort among their own people? And it is not only an instructional campaign that is required. We must deepen the sense of good neighborliness, closer ties between families, irrespective of differences in communal origins or length of stay in Israel . . .

About 300,000 dwellings have been built for immigrants, in addition to those who found homes in existing structures . . . Efforts have been made to give larger dwellings to larger families, but there has been overcrowding among large families—which means, again, mainly among immigrants from Asia and Africa . . . Considerable efforts are now being made to solve the problem by expanding existing homes and more energetic action to clear the slums, in so far as the capacity of our economy permits.

Let me also note the progress made by children of immigrants in the Israel Defense Forces, and the great efforts devoted to providing them with basic education and training for employment, in striking roots in the country. The tremendous value of military service in breaking down barriers between groups of immigrants and communities is obvious . . . The percentage of officers whose parents came from Africa and Asia is rising steadily year by year. Of course there are difficulties, which we shall overcome only with a general rise in educational standards, but today the percentage of platoon commanders coming from these countries is more or less equivalent to their percentage of the population . . .

I am not aware of a single country of immigration that has had to confront a problem of absorption on such a scale and has done so much to tackle it . . . This does not mean that we have achieved all we want. Moreover, the struggles of the early stages have involved difficulties arising out of the measure of progress that has been made. For instance, we are facing the problem of the social absorption of soldiers demobilized from the army. During the years of their service our soldiers become accustomed to a society in which barriers have fallen, but they do not always find the same situation when they return to civil life . . .

I have mentioned the growth of a leadership elite. All of us, all authorities, bodies, associations and parties, must make constant efforts to encourage progress in this sphere. And the idea is not to follow the easy path of developing public activity on a basis of communal labels. This road, which seems deceptively easy, is liable to lead us to demagogic solutions, which cover up the absence of a true solution, with extremist talk or slogans of communal discrimination. The right road is a combination of the efforts of our veteran leaders in public life with the social consolidation of the new immigrant community from within . . .

The communal problem exists not because there is prejudice on the one side and a sense of discrimination, justified or unjustified, on the other. The problem exists because of one grave danger, from which we must not allow our attention to be distracted for a moment: the co-existence in one place of differences of communal origin on the one hand and differences of social and economic standing on the other . . .

Thus, we find that the average monthly income of those born in Asia and Africa who came here after the rise of the State is IL100 lower than that of those born in Europe and America who arrived during the same period. But even immigrants from Europe and America who arrived during the State period have an income of IL200 less than that of those born in Israel.

But I must make two remarks: first, that the general achievement in this sphere is not bad: over IL615 per annum as a national average; and, secondly, that the immigrants from Europe and America who enjoy higher incomes are not only reaping the fruits of their own labor; they are benefiting from the achievements of previous generations, who have provided opportunities of better education not only for them but also for their parents and sometimes their parents' parents as well. If we seriously intend to close this gap, we must realize that it is a task for at least an entire generation.

The economic position naturally has an immediate effect on social status. Again we are not short of encouraging phenomena. The percentage of marriages between persons belonging to different communities is constantly increasing. It has risen from ten per cent in 1952 to almost fifteen per cent ten years later . . .

All of us can see from our personal experience that, to the extent that social differentiation disappears, communal differences steadily lose their significance . . . We must therefore make an extensive effort to solve the social problem, to reduce the gap between social strata and to avoid actions that perpetuate it. . . .

These matters are closely connected with general problems of economic development. The more we achieve in productive development and industrialization, the more paths we open up for social advancement . . . Education and the development of the economy are complementary: new industry needs highly educated employees, while highly educated employees need opportunities of employment in new industries.

We must build our common culture both by means of our attachment to the ancient cultural stratum that is common to all of us and also by drawing from the finest traditions of all Israel's tribes, both in their separateness and in their unity. From this point of view it is most important to foster a consciousness of ourselves, a consciousness of the tradition specific to each community as part of the general consciousness of the Jewish people . . .

By raising educational, social and economic standards, by a meeting of hearts, by cultural contacts, by political representation springing from the ripening of forces from within, combined with natural organic growth—by means of all these things we shall become one people.

Summary of Address at the Tenth Convention of Mapai

February 16, 1965

Immigration Prospects

WITH THE CONTINUED absorption of immigration, we shall have a population of some three million in this country at the end of the decade. Such an immigration will almost exhaust the reservoirs in the lands of distress that are open for emigration; we must therefore show foresight and do all in our power to prepare the ground for immigration from the prosperous countries. We hope we shall see the day when large numbers of our brethren from the Soviet Union will be able to take root in the heritage of their fathers and lend a hand in building the nation's future.

Israel and the Arab Nations

Throughout the life of the State, and also in the near future, we have faced and will continue to face the uncompromising hostility of all the neighboring countries. The novelty that characterizes this hostility today is the transition among the Arabs to long-term planning and the building of a force designed to be decisive in the relatively distant future.

The Arab countries are conducting the struggle against us in three spheres: the building of a military force, an international campaign to damage our prestige and standing, and a plan to sabotage Israel's development by such means as boycott, the stealing of our water, and so forth.

In addition, we must pay heed to ideological developments in the Arab camp, such as the identification of Israel with colonialism. On the one hand, this is a propaganda weapon designed to minimize our influence among the developing nations and coordinate a style of talk with the Soviet Union and China. On the other hand, this identification influences the Arabs themselves and supplies them with a justification for an international struggle without parallel in the annals of disputes between nations, which is aimed at the annihilation of the rival state.

The occasional moderate talk, which is due to acquiescence in the postponement of a decision for a time, is in fact a cover for the most extreme goals. It is not an expression of readiness for peace. This does not mean, of course, that hope is lost forever.

Without undervaluing the gathering hostility and the political successes of those who cherish it, we must not forget the other side of the picture; Nasser's failures in Syria and Yemen and on the economic front. In Yemen, Nasser has invested tens of thousands of soldiers and tremendous resources, without having the power to bring about the decision that he desires.

In the economic area, through his devotion to a policy of rearmament, aggression and grandiose operations, Nasser has brought his country, if not to bankruptcy, then, at any rate, to a catastrophic economic situation and dependence on foreign aid: in a nation of thirty million, one out of every two *pittas* eaten by the Egyptian *fellah* comes from foreign gifts.

These developments may perhaps produce changes in the long run. A generation will arise that will understand that what is needed for Socialism is Socialists, and not ambitious dictators who starve their people and use a foreign-made "socialist" label to stick on the home-made bottle of chauvinistic poison.

Israel's Defense

In view of this situation, the Israel Defense Forces must be equipped and ready to deal suitably with any attack on the borders. The aggressors in the Syrian army have recently learned in their own persons the meaning of this readiness. But no one need cherish the illusion that a more "gentlemanly" aggression, in the form of diversion of water sources, for instance, will not meet with a suitable reaction. We have warned our neighbors on this subject in unambiguous terms.

We still hope that Lebanon will succeed in maintaining her special position in this region, with her democratic culture and her liberal economy. We hope that she will resist being swept away by a negative nationalism, which for Lebanon would mean the abandonment of her own characteristic policy and perhaps even—in the course of time—her independence.

In addition to the capacity for immediate defense, the Israel Defense Forces must have such power that the enemy will be compelled to take their reaction into account and refrain from embarking on any adventure.

I should be happy if I could be confident that the next four years will be as relatively quiet as the past four. For the present, it appears to me that the nation will be called upon to make greater efforts and material sacrifices in order to maintain our army's defensive and deterrent strength.

Israel's International Position

Our enemies are trying to undermine our international position in various ways, but Israel has achievements to her credit: both at the United Nations and in the acquisition of friends among the great powers, among other states, and among scores of developing nations in Asia, Africa, and Latin America.

Our relations with the United States have become closer. This is a continuation of the friendship that has been established over the years with the great American people, and which has found expression in massive and generous aid. I should like, in this connection, to stress the hope that the agreement which exists between us on a matter which we regard as of great and vital importance—the question of water—will stand the test; I am referring both to the utilization of ordinary water resources and their transfer to the places where they are wanted, and also our cooperation in the project for the desalination of sea water.

Another matter that will be tested is the United States' policy of supporting peace in this area, to the extent that this has been shown by her reactions to the race for arms by the Arab states, which are organizing themselves under a joint command in order to attack us. The Arab rulers are trying to exploit the competition between the great powers for this purpose, and some of our friends present the matter as if it makes the slightest difference to us where the bullet comes from that strikes us from across the border. All bullets are equal, and they should not be entrusted to an aggressor.

As for France, I remain confident that there will be no change in the friendship between us. The feelings of fraternity and gratitude which the people of Israel feel for France and her people, because of their support in days of stress and more tranquil times, will be neither obliterated or weakened. My feeling is that the friendship between the two countries has deep roots in the heart of the French people.

In a few weeks I hope to meet Mr. Harold Wilson,

the Prime Minister of Britain. I hope that the friendly statements made by members of the Labor Government have created a basis for understanding in the discussion of affairs and interests. I feel it fitting that a greeting should be sent from the platform of this convention to the British Labor Party, our colleague in the Socialist International, on its return to power.

Yesterday the Knesset devoted a session to the question of our relations with Germany, and I made a statement on behalf of the Government. Our evaluation of the extent to which Germany has cast off her past is tested daily in the light of her deeds in the present. Jewish ethics does not believe in the principle "The fathers have eaten sour grapes and the teeth of the sons are set on edge." But it is the sons themselves who are on trial, and in this respect we can only see an appalling moral weakness in the West German Government's surrender to Arab blackmail.

The Government of Israel cannot accept any excuse for surrender to such blackmail, whether in the area of the boycott, our international status, or aid for Israel's security and economic needs. The talk of "areas of tension" cannot apply to Israel. There is no "area of tension" here. Here there is a peace-loving Israel and states that have threatened her since the day she was established. It is right not to help the aggressor; it is wrong to help him, either with arms or with scientists. But there is no justification for not helping the party marked out to be attacked, in the name of some vague concept that combines the two in the term "areas of tension." This is a moral test and Germany must be sensitive to it.

The Government is endeavoring to advance and improve the dialogue between ourselves and the Soviet Union, as well as with the Eastern bloc in general. What has been achieved in this area is slight, but we shall not lose hope or abandon our efforts.

This is the place for mentioning the disappointment we feel at China's attitude to the State of Israel. We recognize the great and growing importance of China in Asia and in the world at large. To our regret, we have not yet found a readiness in Peking for the establishment of relations.

Of course, we fully support the principle which the Soviet Union presents to the family of nations—absolute abstention from the use of force to change the existing boundaries of sovereign states. Both in public Soviet statements and in talks it has been made clear to us that this rule applies to Israel.

An important chapter in our foreign relations is that of our ties with the developing countries in Africa, Asia and Latin America. In the course of our cooperation in the development of these countries, we have trained some four thousand men and sent hundreds of experts. With all the modesty appropriate to the contribution of a small country like ours to the progress of the awakening world, we may say that we have played a not inconsiderable role and acquired lasting friendships.

The efforts of the Arabs to injure us, including the economic boycott, have so far, in general, failed.

Surrender to the boycott has not paid. We shall have to develop and strengthen our counter-action to this form of aggression, and I am confident that the futility of Arab economic blackmail will become clear to all.

Economic Problems

I must start with a frightening figure: the gap of over five hundred million dollars in our trade balance. On the other hand, however, development continues, individual consumption grows in real terms by 6 per cent per annum, services steadily improve—in short, we are enjoying a prosperity that grows from year to year.

The gap is created as a result of more rapid development and the absorption of mass immigration, which naturally involves investments in housing, services, etc. It is covered by sources of capital which will not always be of the same dimensions, such as appeals, donations, grants, reparations and restitution.

The present situation is liable to continue till approximately the end of this decade, and were it not for our responsibility for what may happen afterwards, we would not need to resist the "natural" processes operating in our economy. The problem that faces us is how to utilize our "seven good years" —actually, less than seven—in such a way that the seven lean years will not follow and eat up the seven good years.

In the case of Joseph in Egypt, the solution was

to accumulate grain. In our case the main solution is to strengthen and develop the economy, to accumulate reserves, sound capital investments, technical and human resources.

In order to do these things, our national product must continue to grow; we have already attained a rate of growth which is one of the highest in the world: more than ten per cent a year. For this purpose, we must slow down the rate of increase in personal consumption and public expenditure. We must decide, as our objective, that the rate of growth in the next four or five years should be around not more than three per cent. I do not regard that as such a grave sacrifice: we have already reached an average European rate of income—some $900 per capita per annum.

If we do not adopt such measures, we are liable, in another four or five years, to reach a trade deficit of $750 million and consume all our reserves, which at the moment total some $500 million. If we do take the necessary action, our reserves will remain intact at the end of the decade, while the trade deficit will fall to three or four hundred million dollars a year, if not less.

The main feature of our settlement in this country has been our return to the soil, and in this respect we have reached a certain degree of saturation. The continuance of our consolidation will, therefore, depend first and foremost on industrialization. This does not mean that we need not continue to develop agriculture. New settlement will continue in Galilee, the Korazim area, the Besor area and the Arava.

Towards the end of the decade we must achieve

total exports of 1,600 to 1,700 million dollars a year—almost double our present exports—and almost all the increase will come from industry.

By the nature of things, and also as the result of a deliberate effort, the benefits of development will also accrue to our Arab and Druse population. We want to see them completely integrated in the country's economy and social structure.

Immigration and Relations with World Jewry

By the end of the decade, as I have said, we may exhaust the reservoirs of immigration from the lands of distress. But immigration from the prosperous countries, comparable in dimensions with the previous rate of immigration, will not begin all of a sudden, overnight, on the first of January 1971, unless we foster this immigration gradually during the years we have left until that date.

From now on, we must devote effort and thought to the education of Diaspora Jewry and the fostering of its attachment to Israel. This is the true meaning of the watchword "Facing the Diaspora" as it applies to the State of Israel.

Educational Problems

The educational part of our work can be approached from various angles: from the point of view of security, the development of the economy and the country, the cultural and social unity of our people in its land, and the unity of the Jewish people the world over. Our cultural and scientific development in the world of the last third of the twentieth century depends first of all on education in all stages, from the kindergarten up to general and technical higher education.

The conclusions of the special committee on the raising of the compulsory school age by a further year have recently been published, and we shall have to devote time and energy to the discussion that has already started on one aspect of the question.

About one-third of the students in the post-primary schools are already exempt from tuition fees, and we believe that in the course of time we shall arrive at post-primary education for all. Nor must we neglect the other end of the scale. We are already covering half the three-year-old and four-year-old age-groups requiring free kindergarten education. In the next few years we shall cover them all.

Our school population has grown sixfold, while the total population has grown only threefold. Our educational system must continue to grow at a higher rate than the total population.

We have twenty thousand students in our universities, in addition to some six thousand in teachers' colleges. The Government expects that the number of university students will be doubled by the end of the decade, while the population will grow only by one-fifth. A Government committee is considering the question of higher education.

Development of Science

We have research institutions in this country which constitute a suitable framework for basic research, but there is a shortage of institutions capable of absorbing their ideas and transforming them into a contribution to the economy; the intermediate links between science and industry are lacking. We must devote our efforts to revealing the possibilities that the new scientific situation offers us.

This question is connected with our social ideal. We want a covenant between the manual worker and the professional worker. In the new pioneering industries the scientists, the engineers, the expert and the technician are the backbone of the enterprise.

We may be permitted to envision a kibbutz almost all of whose members are scientists, engineers and technicians. We can foresee the possibility that groups of Jewish scientists and technologists, from Israel and abroad, will organize themselves to establish new industries in the form of cooperative groups, owning the enterprise, without having to set aside profits for capital, and thus increasing our capacity to penetrate into foreign markets.

This does not mean shackling the progress of private enterprise; nor does it exempt us from the effort to attract productive private capital, combined with initiative and skill, to increase industrialization and technical development. Such capital will receive every assistance.

The workers of Israel must be conscious, in all fields, of the importance of science and research for our development. We must realize the vital importance of scientific development as a prior condition for the achievements of the great goals we set ourselves: the expansion of the population, economic independence, the settlement of the wastelands, and the consolidation of Israel's security.

Statement in the Knesset Concerning Diplomatic Relations with the German Federal Republic

---

March 16, 1965

ON MARCH 7, the German Government announced its decision to establish diplomatic relations with Israel. On the same day Chancellor Erhard sent a special envoy to Jerusalem to discuss with the Government of Israel the complex of problems pending between Israel and the German Federal Republic.

Last Sunday, March 14, the Government of Israel decided to accept the German Federal Republic's proposal for the immediate establishment of diplomatic relations with Israel.

I have the honor to bring this decision to the attention of the Knesset.

The decision of the German Federal Government was preceded by grave developments, which made the problem of the relations between Germany and Israel one of our principal concerns.

While we were engaged in a grave debate over the German scientists in Egypt and endeavoring to prevent the hiring of German technological skill to Israel's enemies, while the Jewish people was in the midst of a controversy with Germany over the abolition of the statute of limitations for Nazi crimes, we were shocked by the German Government's decision to stop the fulfilment of obligations it had undertaken in regard to various security matters—a decision adopted in openly declared response to the President of Egypt's blackmail and threats against Germany.

The Government, the Knesset and the nation in Israel reacted vigorously. We expressed our opposition and protest in dignified and considered terms to the German people and the world at large. We refused to agree to accept "compensation." That does not meet the point of principle involved in the situation. We regarded Germany as confronted with a historic test, as burdened with the moral duty of displaying and proving her desire to atone for the period of total eclipse under the Nazi regime.

In these circumstances, I said in the Knesset on February 15: "The whole of civilized humanity tends to judge and evaluate the extent to which Germany has liberated herself from the burden of the past by her actions in the sphere of relations with Israel and the Jewish people. It is also natural to regard Germany's policy towards Israel as the touchstone for her aspiration to find her place in the family of nations as a factor for world peace and stability."

Here I must state that the more we have tried to establish closer ties with the new Europe, the more clearly we have realized the considerable importance of Germany in the European community.

Our aspiration to strengthen Israel's position within the new European fabric and the need to encourage resistance to our neighbor's blackmail obligate us to adopt a clear and affirmative decision.

Dr. Birrenbach, Chancellor Erhard's special envoy, will return to Israel tomorrow to complete the discussions started ten days ago. In parallel with a settlement of the matter of diplomatic relations, he will discuss with us the complex of problems in regard to which both governments have expressed their desire to reach mutual understanding. There is reason to hope that we shall succeed in arriving at an agreed settlement.

I know that the decision required of us today is no mere matter of routine. It cannot be compared with the establishment of diplomatic relations with any other country. Many of us are engrossed in a struggle between emotion and reason.

The account of conscience and history which emerges from the holocaust lies far beyond the limits of any political act, but even that account, unparalleled in gravity, cannot exempt us from the duty of carrying out the central and the decisive task that confronts us in this generation: to consolidate the State of Israel. Our people's past, present, and future imperatively call upon us to increase its material and spiritual strength, so that it may face the trials in store. It is our sacred duty to safeguard Israel's honored status in the family of nations.

It is particularly the memory of the weakness and impotence which characterized the eras of tribulation and disaster in Jewry's annals that obligates us to seize every opportunity to weaken our enemies and ensure a strong and stable foundation for the continued survival of the Jewish people in its homeland.

I am confident that in the balance of reason and emotion, this consideration—the need to strengthen and consolidate the State of Israel—must weigh down the scale.

Broadcast to the Citizens of Israel at the Approach of the Jewish New Year 5727

September 11, 1966

I SHOULD LIKE this evening to take stock together with you—to take stock of the position of the community, of the State. Such a stocktaking is worth while on any day of the year, and particularly at this festive season when we are starting a New Year.

The central aims of our country, I believe, are four in number: peace between ourselves and our neighbors; more Jewish immigration from the Diaspora and the strengthening of our ties with the Jewish communities abroad; the integration of all groups of immigrants into one nation; and progress towards economic independence.

During the past year we have been compelled to repulse further aggressive provocation by our neighbors. We have done so after exercising a large measure of self-restraint, making every effort to prevent or minimize casualties. As in previous years, threats of war against us have come from Damascus and Cairo. In the face of those and similar threats, we must strengthen our military power, which is the principal guarantee for the prevention of war in our area. During the past year we have continued to strengthen this power, while resolutely guarding our sovereignty.

Important developments have taken place during the year in the acquisition of armaments—in the shape of tanks and planes. Israel's water project, which started operations in the summer of 1964, brings a flow of sweet water to the various regions of the country. During the past year we have made it plain to the Arabs by deeds that we shall not permit the diversion of the water resources that are our due. Our neighbors may rest assured that just as we shall be able to stand against any provocation, so we shall continue in the future to honor any agreement between them and us.

The quest for peace; the strengthening of opposition to war, the first signs of which may be witnessed in the Arab world; our vision of peace and cooperation in the Middle East for the benefit of all its peoples—these are central elements in our thoughts and our policy. I believe that this combined policy of strengthening our deterrent power, while seeking ways for dialogue with the Arab world, will bear fruit.

We shall continue to improve our ties with those countries in the world that are interested in friendship and cooperation with us. During my visit to Africa a few months ago, I found a will and a readiness for closer cooperation with Israel on the part of many countries in that continent, the growing independence of which is adding a new dimension to the consciousness of humanity. We have also established closer ties with other areas in the world.

There appear to be possibilities of broadening relations in the economic and cultural spheres with various countries in the Eastern bloc. Despite the disappointments in our relations with the Soviet Union, I do not despair of an improvement in relations with that power.

Evidence of the development of our ties with the countries of the world and the deepening consciousness of the centrality of Jerusalem as our capital was given by the coming of forty-four heads of parliament from all over the globe to celebrate with us the dedication of the Knesset building.

It may be said, I believe, that there was progress in the overall balance of events and developments in the fields of security and international affairs so far as concerned us.

As for immigration and ties with the Jewish dispersion, it is no secret that we have not been blessed with large-scale immigration during the past year. Immigration from the lands of distress is coming to an end, and we look with expectation more and more to the Jews from the prosperous countries. Together with them, we must devote our efforts to the quest for ways of preparing the ground for the arrival and absorption of immigrants. At all times, we remember our brethren who are not permitted to live full Jewish lives, to preserve the Jewish language and culture and pass them on to their children after them, and to come home to us in order to take root on the soil of the Homeland.

We must strengthen the bridge between Israel and the Diaspora and deepen the sense of Jewish identity everywhere as a bulwark against assimilation and disintegration. We must increase the stream of Jewish youth, pioneers and others—students at universities, secondary schools, and Yeshivoth—coming to settle in Israel, to visit the country, or to study here. Jewish education of all kinds in the Diaspora needs fostering. This must be a common task for all our people, whether they live in Israel or in the Diaspora. Let it not be said—Heaven forbid—that we have established a State and lost a people.

Coming to the question of the unity of our people in Israel which is bound up with the question of education, we must admit that the work is harder than we imagined and that there is still a long way before we reach complete integration. This problem will not be solved by mere slogans. The challenge is great, and there is much work still ahead of us.

We must persevere in our efforts to abolish the dangerous gap in education between brethren from the Western and the Oriental countries. We must continue to improve the organization of all types and levels of our educational system to bring about the integration of the communities and the unity of the nation in Israel.

The main part of my remarks this evening I shall devote to economic affairs.

It may be that this year marks a turning point in our economic life, especially in the feelings of the public about this question. The truth, which we have repeatedly emphasized over the years, has begun to penetrate to the consciousness of our people. At last we are beginning to understand that all of us, the community and the individual, have been maintaining a standard of life beyond the capacity of the economy, beyond our natural and other resources.

During the past few years, the economy has expanded rapidly; every year production has grown by 10 per cent and exports by tens of millions of pounds. We have found work for tens and hundreds of thousands of immigrants. But despite all these achievements—and they are numerous—we have not succeeded in providing productive employment to the extent that would enable us to achieve economic independence.

We have achieved full employment—even over-employment—and perhaps that is the reason why we have been unable to ensure that the employment should be productive and permanent. Our exports have risen rapidly, but imports have grown as well, and the gap between them has not shrunk.

It is true that we have succeeded in increasing production, thanks to donations, investments and loans—and thanks also to the flow of immigration—but only part of this growth has been utilized for productive investment and exports.

Too large a part of our production has been utilized to bring about too rapid a rise in our standard of living—a rise unparalleled anywhere in the world. We have permitted ourselves exaggerated increases in expenditures, profits, and wages. We have managed with low productivity, faulty management, and inefficient organization. We have permitted ourselves ostentatious spending, inflated staffs and managements, and a superfluous growth in the number of employees in enterprises and undertakings, public and private. All of us—from professional men and managers to laborers—have permitted ourselves to demand of the economy more and more rises in wages and incomes. All this has been at the expense of employment for export.

Many thousands have been employed in work that could have been dispensed with, or done with less manpower or expenditure. Some have received wages and profits out of all proportion to their effective contribution to the economy. Industries working for the domestic market have increased their production, while export industries, on which our survival depends, have been unable to develop adequately, because their competitive capacity has been affected by the rise in production costs, and the booming domestic market did away with the will and the need to increase exports.

We have exhorted the people and warned that these developments would have grave results; we have demanded self-restraint, but our call has gone unanswered. The Government has, therefore, decided to take steps on its part to prevent the continuation of the process. We have initiated measures to moderate the rate of the rise in the standard of living and to direct resources to investments and exports.

Possibly, it is true, we could have continued for a few years more with the race to increase the standard of living. In such a case the Government might even have enjoyed a temporary popularity, but at the end of these years we should have arrived at a serious crisis. The Government has chosen the hard way and has started to put things right in good time. We still have in our possession reserves amounting to hundreds of millions of dollars, which will make it easier for us to alter the situation of the economy without hurting too much.

The Government started its policy of restraint last year. Measures of economy and efficiency were initiated in the Government Ministries, and some of them should be extended to the whole of the economy, to every institution and undertaking.

In the meantime, to our regret, immigration has shrunk and the need for new building has diminished. These changes have slowed down the growth of domestic demand, and they liberate commodities and labor for the expansion of exports.

This development is useful in itself, but it lays bare the points of weakness in our economy. The first and gravest of them is concealed unemployment, which has now become revealed.

Our main concern is for the individual man or woman. He is our principal asset. In his hands lies the solution to the problems of the economy. It is our duty to see to it that every individual will be able to work, earn a decent living and contribute to the country's progress.

The road to a fundamental solution of the employment problems is the expansion of production for export. Only in this way can we ensure full, stable and productive employment. The more efficient and the cheaper our production the more men we shall be able to employ in industry and other export branches, in order to diminish the gap and reduce our dependence on external aid.

The Histadrut responded to our appeal and in order to prevent an increase in production costs—and in unemployment—decided not to demand the payment of an increased cost-of-living allowance in July. This was a proof of responsibility for the economy and for the worker. It is true that the declared aim of the cost-of-living allowance is to compensate the workers for increased prices, but it also undoubtedly increases production costs and prices.

Let me point out at this stage that, even after this act of self-denial, the level of real wages is still higher than it was two years or a year ago.

Today the Government has decided on a series of further steps of self-restraint on the part of the community and the individual. It has undertaken to work for price stability. It will abstain from imposing new taxation. It will encourage investments and work for the fuller exploitation of existing production capacity in the various sections of the economy. It will make its services more efficient. It will continue to make every effort to economize in its expenditures and those of all public institutions.

Further efforts will be made to prevent profiteering. We shall take vigorous steps to ensure the honest payment of taxes and to reduce exemptions for business expenses. The tax on capital profits will be increased and measures will be taken to cut bank commissions. The Government will grant incentives to encourage exports and increase their profitability.

The measures I have enumerated are designed to

bring down the cost of production and services, to absorb more workers and combat unemployment. I have reason to believe that the Histadrut, taking a realistic view of the economic position and the needs of the workers, will also conduct a policy of self-restraint and the consolidation of the economy. It will help by investigating production norms, adapting them to the changes that have taken place in the economy through the introduction of additional equipment and the workers' acquisition of greater skill in their work. It will endeavor to increase productivity and reduce production costs. It will respond to our demand to waive half the cost-of-living allowance increase during the next two years—except for family men with low incomes, who will receive full compensation for price rises.

These measures will help us to solve the two interdependent problems: the problem of employment and the problem of exports. The principle is this: The more exports, the more productive employment.

It is obvious that until industry, agriculture and the other export branches are able to absorb the workers who are paid off in building services, there will be a difficult transition period for thousands and perhaps tens of thousands. The Government on its part will make great efforts to ensure that the transition shall be brief and rapid.

The battle-ground of economic policy consists of the enterprises themselves. Only increased productivity and more effort will bring down the cost of production and make it profitable. Only increased competitive capacity will increase employment.

Thanks to our efforts we are fortunate today in possessing a powerful production machine, which is capable of absorbing thousands of additional workers, if only we succeed in bringing down production costs and winning foreign markets. I am confident that production can be made more efficient, and output per employee increased by 20 or 30 per cent, without calling upon managements and men for efforts beyond their capacity. Such an increase in output would bring us up to the European level of production and open up new markets.

I believe that our call today will meet with a ready hearing. The success of the plan depends on each and every one of us. It is clear to everyone that if these measures do not suffice, more radical ones will be inevitable. I am confident that the entire nation understands the challenge; I am confident that we shall be able to face it.

Finally: I know that each and every one of us shares in the aspirations I have expressed this evening. May we be able to master the inner strength to follow the road we have marked out for ourselves, so that the year 5727 may be a year of blessing for all of us!

Good night and a Happy New Year.

Broadcast on Remembrance Day for Those Who Fell in Defense of Israel

May 13, 1967

ON THE EVE of the nineteenth Remembrance Day for the Israel Defense Forces combatants who fell in Israel's battles, the nation bows its head in grief—with gratitude and pride in its heart.

The history of our people everywhere is replete with blood and tears. It always had to struggle hard for its right to exist, and many are its victims and its martyrs. But since we were exiled from our land, with the destruction of the Second Temple, there has never been an epoch similar to the years of struggle for the establishment of the State and the fight for its existence—a period when those who fell knew so well the reason and the purpose of their fight. In the words of the poet: "Brothers! Perhaps once in a thousand years our death has meaning." They fought for their State and in the name of their State. There is no consolation for the blood spilled, but the very knowledge that this blood was shed for the living provides it with significance. It is a source of pride for fathers and mothers, wives and husbands, sons and daughters. It is the source of gratitude of the entire nation which knows full well that the fighters and the fallen have bequeathed to it their testament of life.

All of us, the Government of Israel, the Defense Forces of Israel, and the entire people stand in mute homage in front of the ever-fresh graves. In our hearts we pray that the sword will no longer prevail in our midst and that we shall not have to wield it in war.

This prayer was not granted last year. We are still surrounded by a wall of enmity, even though some cracks have appeared in it. We are still obliged to defend our borders, our very lives, our rights and our honor. In the past year fifteen soldiers have lost their lives, members of the Border Police and of border villages. To the bereaved families go our condolences in their profound grief, and to the wounded, our best wishes for a speedy recovery.

During the past year we have made great strides ahead for the strengthening and consolidation of the State of Israel. The firm and persistent stand we have taken on behalf of our rights has strengthened the awareness among our neighbors that they will not be able to prevail against us in open combat. They recoil today from any frontal clash with Israel and they postpone the date of such a confrontation to the remote future. Among the Arab rulers and their saboteur-minions there are some who *nowadays* attempt to manifest their hostility to Israel in deeds, diligently in search of ways of attrition, subversion and aggression against human lives. We have furnished proof that we shall not permit our borders to be opened to attack. We have proved that to their attempts to pick easy and exposed targets, we were able to respond at a place, time and by a method of *our own* choosing. Thus, the saboteurs and their employers found out that they would not accomplish their aims this way. We do not recognize the limitations they endeavor to impose upon our acts of response. The Arab states and the nations of the world ought to know that any border which is tranquil from their side—will also be quiet from our side, and if they will try to sow unrest on our border —unrest will come to theirs.

Citizens of Israel!

In addition to the security front line, we have continued during the past year to weather the trials on the economic front of upbuilding the country. Immigration has shrunk. Capital imports have decreased. The Government has taken energetic measures in order to consolidate the economy and to progress towards economic independence. We knew we would not be able in the future to continue raising our standard of living at its past rate of increase. If in the past there may have been some reason for a rapid rise in living standards, since we integrated a massive and impecunious immigration, everybody admits that today there is no justification for it. The road upon which we have embarked is a hard one. We all must know that from now on the effort will be ours for many years to come, so that we shall stand on our own feet economically, and consolidate and expand our economy, absorbing into it all those seeking work today—and those who will come to us as immigrants.

The Government embarked upon this road with open eyes, fully aware of the difficulties involved. It has also given a clear warning of its intentions. It has not chosen an easy road. We knew full well that this policy would cause hardship and suffering to those thousands of workers compelled to change jobs and go from work keyed to the local market to work for exports. We have done, and continue to do, everything in order to make sure these difficulties are temporary. However, it is important that every citizen should know and understand that the duration of the transition period depends entirely upon us, the citizens of Israel. The one way to supply employment-seekers with steady and productive work, is production for export. The quicker we shall increase productivity, streamline enterprises and the economic system, shrink production costs and economize—the faster our competitiveness will grow, the more exports and investments will increase and more workers will be absorbed by enterprises. This is the Government's test—the test of the entire nation.

Indeed, our activities are already bearing their first fruits. In recent months a growth in production and in exports has been felt. Prices are stabilizing and productivity has grown. The Government has even anticipated the implementation of development works, in order to avert an increase in unemployment during the transition period. But here I wish to warn against placidity and complacency. The road is still long and much labor still lies ahead of us. We all must display initiative, diligence and dedication. The worker and the industrialist, the clerk and the waiter, the farmer and the pilot, the physician and the scientist, the engineer and the economist—all can, and must, strive and show initiative for the development of our national economy, so that it will stand on its own feet and be prepared to absorb further immigrants from the countries of affluence, as well as the countries of hardship and silence.

Our primary obligation was and is the absorption of immigrants. Today immigration has shrunk. Some of its reservoirs have dwindled, and great Jewish communities still have their gates closed. We are hopeful and must make efforts so that Jews should be able to come from wherever they reside. We must strive for the complete and full integration of those immigrants who have already arrived, irrespective of whether they came fifteen or ten years ago, or quite recently. It is our duty towards ourselves and to our future that every immigrant will find not only a roof and a job, but also a warm home and open hearts. Thus we shall bring about an increase in immigration, and thorough integration. This is a task for all of us as well as the duty of every single one in our midst, wherever he may meet immigrants, particularly new arrivals. Let us all live up to this duty which is our privilege.

Those who fell gave their lives so that there should rise the State of Israel, the Jewish State; so that it should be strong, stable and live by the labor and the spiritual creation of its citizens. That it be open to every Jew and attract all Jews. Be it granted that we shall prove worthy of those who fell—and of their supreme sacrifice.

Statement at the Opening of the Summer Session of the Knesset

---

May 22, 1967

MR. CHAIRMAN, MEMBERS OF THE KNESSET:

This session of the Knesset opens against the background of grave developments which took place during the past week on Egypt's border with Israel. I shall briefly review the chain of events.

During the night of May 15, 1967, news of the movement of Egyptian military forces into Sinai reached us from various sources. Military forces had been openly and demonstratively transferred, in broad daylight. Cairo explained that this step was taken in response to Israel's alleged preparations to attack Syria, and concentration of military forces on the northern frontier.

Upon learning of the Egyptian troop movements and the pretext offered to explain them, and before Egyptian forces had crossed the Suez Canal, we informed the UN that the allegations of Israeli troop concentrations in northern Israel were baseless. This statement was released for publication in the world press. Indeed, our statement was transmitted by the UN to Middle Eastern capitals, including Cairo. In his report to the Security Council on May 19, 1967, the UN Secretary-General states that UN observers verified the absence of Israeli troop concentrations and Israeli military movements on the northern frontier.

Nevertheless, Egyptian troop movements continued in the direction of Sinai, while mendacious propaganda continued to proceed from Cairo and Damascus concerning Israeli concentrations which had never taken place.

During the first days of Egyptian troop movements towards Sinai, authoritative political circles in the world capitals expressed the view that this was merely a propaganda move, devoid of any particular military significance.

The movement of Egyptian forces into Sinai gathered strength during the second half of last week, and today they are almost fully deployed in Eastern Sinai and various positions throughout the Peninsula. Before May 14, the Egyptian force in Sinai consisted of less than two divisions, based mainly on infantry and some armor. Today, after reinforcements, Egyptian forces there are of a strength of close to four divisions of armored infantry. Furthermore, numerous artillery units have been brought up, and the Palestinian forces in the Gaza Strip have been strengthened. Moreover, the Egyptian air force in the Sinai Peninsula has also been reinforced.

All in all, the strength of Egyptian forces in Sinai has grown, according to our estimate, from 35,000 to 80,000 men. This is the first time that Egypt has brought forces of such dimensions into Sinai. With the increase of the Egyptian force and its advance into east Sinai, a graver international view is also being taken of Egypt's likely intentions and possible moves.

Members of the House:

While Egyptian forces advanced into east Sinai, the chief of staff of Egypt's armed forces informed the commander of the UN Emergency Force on Tuesday, May 16, as follows:

> "I have instructed all the armed forces of the United Arab Republic to be ready for action against Israel, as soon as Israel carries out any aggressive action against any Arab state. In the light of these instructions, our forces have already been concentrated in Sinai on our eastern border. In order to ensure the full safety of all UN forces deployed in observation posts along our borders, we request that the removal of these forces be ordered at once."

The commander of the UN Emergency Force replied that he would at once report accordingly to the UN Secretary-General since he had no authority to withdraw any parts of the UN Emergency Force or to alter their deployment in any manner, unless instructed to do so by the Secretary-General.

From then on matters were dealt with by the UN Secretary-General. U Thant at once requested clarifications from the Egyptian representative at the UN, but at the same time he saw fit, for some reason, to announce on his own initiative that any request for the temporary removal of the UN Emergency Force from the border would be regarded as a demand for the complete evacuation of the force from the Gaza Strip and Sinai.

The UN Secretary-General's announcement was soon followed on the very same day, by Egypt's official request for the complete evacuation of the UN Force from Egyptian territory and from the Gaza Strip.

The Secretary-General pointed out, it is true, in his reply on the same day, that the evacuation of the force was liable to be of grave significance for the peace of the region, but to the general surprise, on the other hand, he complied at once with the request for evacuation.

On Friday, May 19, the commander of the UN Force, General Rikhye, informed the Israeli authorities that, as from 4:00 P.M. of the same day, the force had ceased to carry out its functions and that it would remain in its bases and act only to ensure its own safety. This is the *only* official communication on this subject which Israel has received from the UN. Here I must point out that Israel was a party to this international arrangement, reached in 1957, but the Secretary-General did not see fit to consult Israel before he adopted his hasty decision.

Members of the House:

The UN Emergency Force was established by virtue of the General Assembly resolution of November 5, 1956. For more than ten years this force, consisting of soldiers of many countries, was deployed in Sinai—at Kuntila and Sharm-a-Sheikh and in the Gaza Strip.

The function of this force, according to the UN General Assembly resolution of February 8, 1957, was to contribute to the maintenance of peaceful conditions in the region. In other words, its establishment was based upon the aspiration to prevent hostilities and promote the transition from belligerency to peace. The UN Force was not intended, it is true, nor was it physically able, to prevent a clash between the parties. The very fact of its presence in certain areas—and the tasks it actually fulfilled—constituted, no doubt, a positive factor.

The UN Force was deployed in its positions in our region for more than ten years. The demand for its evacuation, and the compliance with it, undoubtedly involve a weakening of the UN's position in its functions of keeping the peace.

It is noteworthy that even at the time when UNEF was established, the question of how the UN would act and react in case of an Egyptian demand for its evacuation was raised. In his memorandum of February 26, 1957, the then Secretary-General, Dag Hammerskold, reported to the General Assembly on a statement which he had transmitted to the Government of Israel, in which he said that suitable procedure would be for the Secretary-General to inform the advisory committee of UNEF (of the demand for evacuation), while the committee would decide whether to bring the demand to the attention of the General Assembly. As far as we know, the present Secretary-General, U Thant, did not submit the demand for a decision by the advisory committee prior to adopting his decision and, of course, the General Assembly was not enabled to consider the demand for evacuation.

It is known that several member-states of the advisory committee have expressed objections to the step taken by the Secretary-General in this matter. Israel had every reason to believe that any demand for the withdrawal of this force would be considered at length and in good time, so as to clarify all the consequences that the evacuation demand would entail.

Mr. Speaker, Members of the House:

The latest development is a link in a chain of tension, the source of which lies in Damascus. From this rostrum I have already dwelt upon the fact that Syria has been alone in her demands to wage war at once against Israel, and in this connection has initiated the organization of bands of saboteurs and assassins to operate on Israeli territory.

From 1965 up to May 1967, 113 minelaying and sabotage attempts and operations have been perpetrated on Israeli soil for which Syria is responsible —whether they came directly from her territory or via the territory of other countries. In addition, scores of shooting and shelling outrages against Israeli farmers have been initiated from Syrian territory, including the shelling of villages.

Since July 1966 we have complained to the UN of such Syrian operations in thirty-four notes to the Security Council, as well as maintaining constant contact with the UN Secretariat and the chief of the UN observers in the region on the subject.

These sabotage operations were accompanied by announcements, threats, and bellicose statements made by Syrian leaders. Hand in hand with this activity, Syria has made the foolish claim that it was Israel, as it were, which was about to attack her. This past week was not the first time that Syrian sources spread mendacious reports of large-scale Israeli troop concentrations on the northern border for the purpose of attacking her.

Four times during the past two years the chief of the UN observers suggested a check on both sides of the border in connection with the allegations of threatening troop concentrations.

On March 17, 1965, the chief of UN observers proposed a review on the borders. Next day, Israel replied in the affirmative, while Syria failed to reply at all, and no check took place.

On June 3, 1966, the UN made a similar request. Both sides agreed and the check was carried out.

On October 19, 1966, when the Syrians repeated their allegations, Israel, on her own initiative, proposed that the chief of UN observers should again carry out a similar check, which, indeed, took place.

On April 15 of this year, when Arab elements and others spread rumors of heavy Israeli troop concentrations, deployed for attack, the chief of the UN observers suggested to both parties that another check be carried out by him. On April 18, Israel expressed her consent. The check was not carried out owing to the attitude of Syria.

Furthermore, after Syria had not enabled the implementation of such a check during the first week of May, she also failed to respond to the suggestion of the chairman of the Israel-Syria mixed armistice commission to obtain confirmation of the absence of Syrian troop concentrations on her border. Israel replied affirmatively to this request on the very same day.

To sum up: on May 15, the Egyptians explained that they had introduced their forces into Sinai on the strength of Syria's claim of alleged Israeli troop concentrations, deployed for an attack on Syria. In reality, however, Syria did all she possibly could in previous weeks to frustrate every UN endeavor to verify the true state of affairs, lest the spuriousness of her claims be revealed.

Indeed, the Secretary-General in his report to the Security Council of May 19, said, and I quote:

> "The Government of Israel has confirmed to me a few days ago that no unusual concentrations of Israeli forces or unusual military movements have taken place on the Syrian armistice line."

The Secretary-General goes on to say:

> "The reports of UN observers have verified the absence of troop concentrations and the absence of noteworthy military movements on both sides of the line."

Thus it transpires beyond any doubt that the Syrians have spread mendacious rumors which the Egyptians have clutched at and relied upon.

In the face of Syrian aggression we have tried, in

vain, to exhaust all political measures of restraint. When acts of aggression continued and increased in gravity, we considered it necessary in certain cases to exercise our right of self-defense.

Nineteen incursions into Israel have taken place during the past six weeks. The UN Secretary-General himself, in his report to the Security Council of May 19, points out that these acts of terrorism and sabotage by El Fatah are a major factor in the deterioration of the situation to an unusual degree of tension and danger. "These acts provoke strong reactions in Israel by Government and people alike," he said.

This appraisal is of great value for the comprehension of the basic causes of the growing tension in our region of late.

The Secretary-General goes on to state that several incidents have of late apparently indicated a new level of organization and training by those perpetrating sabotage and terrorist activities.

Members of the House:

The tension prevailing between Israel and the Arab countries has been influenced throughout the years by the state of inter-Arab relations and the relationship between the powers—against the background of their global and regional policies. All these factors are inextricably linked with each other.

In view of the mounting tension of late, the big powers ought to exercise their full influence in order to remove the danger of a conflagration in the Middle East.

Particular responsibility rests with the Soviet

Union, which has friendly relations in Damascus and in Cairo, and which has not yet clearly dissociated herself from the policy of Damascus vis-à-vis Israel. It is only fitting that the declared policy of Soviet Russia—which advocates the settlement of controversies by negotiation, and not by violence—should also find expression in our region, without discrimination. This would further the maintenance of peace.

The concentrations of Egyptian forces in Sinai have reached proportions which increase the tension in our region and arouse world concern. The status quo must be restored on both sides of the border.

In the wake of the statements made by the UN Secretary-General, it is incumbent on UN members, and the big powers in particular, to declare in unmistakable terms their strongest opposition to the acts of sabotage carried out against a member state of the UN and to demand the complete cessation of such acts, which are contrary to international law and to the principles of the UN Charter.

International influence should be exerted to its utmost to ensure continuation of the quiet which prevailed on the Egyptian-Israeli border since March 1957, by respecting the vital national and international rights of all states including Israel.

The Secretary-General of the United Nations is leaving tonight for the Middle East, in order to contribute to the relaxation of tension and the consolidation of peace. We shall follow this visit, and its results, with interest.

I would like to say again to the Arab countries

from this rostrum, particularly to Egypt and Syria, that we harbor no aggressive designs. We have no possible interest in violating either their security, their territory, or their legitimate rights. Nor shall we interfere in any way in their internal affairs, their regimes, or their regional or international relations. We expect of them, according to the principles of reciprocity, the application of the same principles towards us.

Members of the Knesset:

During the early days of the movement of Egyptian forces towards Sinai, the view was expressed in various world capitals that it was a question of a purely demonstrative operation of no military significance. Others, of course, can adopt one interpretation or another, but we, to whose frontiers this force has approached, took the view that it was our duty to adopt all necessary steps to meet any possible development.

In view of the Egyptian concentrations on our borders and the evacuation of the UN forces, I ordered a limited mobilization of reserves, which has been carried out according to plan.

On the completion of the limited mobilization, I visited the Israel Defense Forces units. The remarkable capacity of our army, which has been fostered and perfected over the years, has reached a high level today. The Israel Defense Forces are capable today of meeting any test, with the same devotion, skill and capacity that they have demonstrated more than once in the past—and, knowing the facts as I do, I could say even more.

In conclusion, I call upon all the peoples of the Middle East for reciprocal respect for the sovereignty, integrity, and international rights of each of our countries. Israel, with complete confidence in her defensive capacity and her steadfastness of strength and spirit, expresses at this hour her readiness to participate in an effort to reinforce stability and advance peace in our region.

And indeed, what is at stake is a clear and formal international undertaking, on compliance with which the maintenance of international law and order depends. Hence, we are confronted with a fateful hour not only for Israel, but for the whole world. In view of this situation I call upon the powers once again to act without delay for the maintenance of the right to free passage to our southernmost port, a right which applies to every state without distinction. The Government of Israel will adhere to the policy which it announced in the UN Assembly on March 1, 1957. Since this statement was made, free passage in the Strait and the Gulf has taken shape during the past ten years as a well-rooted international reality, expressed in the form of hundreds of sailings under dozens of flags and the creation of a variegated and developing network of commerce and communications.

The illegal statement of the Egyptian President is another link in the violation of law that Egypt has been maintaining for many years by imposing a blockade in the Suez Canal, in violation of its undertakings to permit free passage through the Canal to all ships of all nations.

Members of the Knesset:

In my statement yesterday I called upon the nations of the Middle East for reciprocal respect of the territorial integrity, political sovereignty and rights of all states in the area. I announced Israel's readiness to participate in an effort for the relaxation of tension and the consolidation of peace in our area.

If a criminal attempt is made to impose a blockade on the shipping of a member-state of the United Nations, that will be a dangerous precedent, with grave consequences for international relations and the freedom of these seas. The latest development clearly demonstrates the dangerous significance of Egypt's moves. I call upon international factors to demonstrate practical and effective responsibility for the preservation of peace.

I shall give further details to the Foreign Affairs and Security Committee and we shall continue to consider them. The debate in the Knesset has demonstrated the unity of the nation in meeting the future, with unity and a spirit of alertness and confidence in our midst, we shall meet the days to come.

Statement in the Knesset

May 23, 1967

AT THIS GRAVE hour, I have no intention of replying in detail to all the things that have been said in the debate. From the speeches and the inter-party consultations I have held today, I have gained the impression that the Knesset is united in its views and its will. The events of the past day make it necessary for me to be content with a brief statement on one single subject.

This morning a statement by the Egyptian President was published declaring his intention to block the international waterway which passes through the Strait of Tiran and joins the Gulf of Eilat with the Red Sea to the passage of Israeli flagships and ships of other flags whose cargoes are of a strategic character.

Members of the Knesset:

Any interference with freedom of passage in the Gulf and the Strait constitutes a gross violation of international law, a blow at the sovereign rights of other nations and an act of aggression against Israel.

As the Knesset is aware, a number of governments, including the major maritime powers, have publicly stated, since 1957, their intention of exercising their rights to free passage through the Strait of Tiran and the Gulf of Eilat.

During the past few days, the Government of Israel has been in close touch with the governments that have proclaimed and exercised principle of free passage in these waters since 1967. After these exchanges, I can say that international support for these rights is serious and widespread.

Statement in the Knesset

May 29, 1967

MR. SPEAKER, MEMBERS OF THE KNESSET:

Following upon my statement to the Knesset last week about the security situation, I shall survey the main developments that have taken place in the area:

Two weeks ago, the Egyptian army began to move its concentrations towards eastern Sinai, opposite Israel's frontier. Today the main part of the Egyptian army is concentrated, in battle order, in this area. On our northern frontier, Syria, Egypt's ally, is concentrating its army.

Parallel with this concentration, the United Nations Emergency Force has been hastily evacuated from Sinai, the Gaza Strip, and Sharm-a-Sheikh. This force, which was established by the UN, entered Sinai and the Gaza Strip at the time as part of an arrangement with Israel for the evacuation of her forces from Sinai and the Gaza Strip. This evacuation was carried out on the basis of clear international undertakings for free passage in the Gulf of Aqaba and the cessation of infiltration from the Gaza Strip. The withdrawal of the UN force marks the removal of the symbol of the relative quiet that has reigned on the southern border for the past ten years.

The UN force constituted an expression of the will of the international community to ensure quiet on the border and free passage in the Strait. Nasser's agreement to the force's remaining in Sinai and the Strip expressed for ten years Egypt's readiness to undertake to preserve quiet on her border with Israel and to refrain from interference with free passage in the Strait.

A week ago, the ruler of Egypt, Col. Nasser, announced the closing of the Strait to Israeli shipping and ships carrying cargo to Israel. Since then, he has several times repeated this statement and threats against anyone who should try to break this illegal blockade.

The Egyptian President has further proclaimed his intention and readiness to attack Israel for the purpose of destroying her. Yesterday he went further, and threatened to begin at once with extensive sabotage operations against Israel, her towns and villages, and her citizens. This very day, attacks have been carried out against us from the Gaza Strip.

These acts and declarations have altered the security and political situation in the area. The Government of Israel has, therefore, adopted a number of security and political initiatives with the aim of safeguarding Israel's vital interests.

A pre-condition for safeguarding peace and our interests is our military strength. I therefore ordered, with the Government's agreement, the mobilization of the reserves of the Israel Defense Forces, and they are ready and prepared today to frustrate the enemy's designs in all sectors and on all our borders.

Members of the Knesset:

The Government of Israel has repeatedly stated its determination to exercise its freedom of passage in the Strait of Tiran and the Gulf of Aqaba, and to defend it in case of need. This is a supreme national interest on which no concession is possible and no compromise is admissible. It is clear to us—and I feel that it is now clear to the nations of the world—that so long as the blockade exists, peace is in danger.

It is this grave situation that obligates us particularly to find out first of all and with great urgency whether those governments that have undertaken to support and implement freedom of passage are prepared to translate their undertakings into the language of action in accordance with international law, which the Egyptian ruler so criminally violates.

The Foreign Minister's brief visits to Paris, London, and Washington were designed to clarify this question. He explained to the Presidents of the United States and France and to the British Prime Minister that it was a matter of a vital national interest, which our country will unflinchingly protect. From the Foreign Minister's conversations we learned that all the governments with which he came in contact desired that the status quo, which has recently been violated, should be respected. The President of the United States and the Prime Minister of Britain have made strong public statements on the subject.

There is special interest in the attitude of the

United States, for its government was the first to convey undertakings to Israel in 1957, in diplomatic exchanges, in letters from the President and the Secretary of State, and in public statements in the UN and other places.

After hearing President Johnson's statement of May 23 and the Foreign Minister's report of his talks in Washington, the Government was deeply impressed by the unambiguous stand of the United States in favor of the safeguarding of freedom of passage in these international waters. A similar attitude is expressed by the British Prime Minister, Mr. Harold Wilson, in his public statement and his talks with our Foreign Minister. Other maritime states have already informed us of their readiness to effectively support freedom of passage, and we have been told that practical consultations on the subject are already taking place.

Under these conditions, it is reasonable to expect that the states which support the principle of free passage should carry out and coordinate effective action in order to ensure that the Strait and the Gulf shall be open to the passage of the ships of all nations without discrimination within a short time.

This expectation, which is founded on authorized and express statements, has had a strong influence on the attitude and decisions of the Israel Government at this stage. There is no doubt that the readiness to protect freedom of passage which has been shown by great nations has been influenced both by their attitude in principle and by their knowledge that the State of Israel will protect its rights.

It was our duty first of all to put international undertakings to the test. In the near future it will transpire whether this prospect is being realized. Israel's attitude in regarding the blocking of the Strait as an act of aggression against her remains fully in force. The Israel Government's statement at the United Nations Assembly on March 1, 1957, still expresses our policy with complete accuracy.

We are now engaged in extensive political activity for the restoration of freedom of passage. This activity would not have been possible, and its prospects would have been dim, had it not been for our own strength and the justice of our claim. On the other hand, the ties which we have forged with other nations have helped, and will continue to help, to enhance our strength and protect our rights.

Members of the Knesset:

The Egyptian ruler's statements about the closing of the Strait, about acts of violence, about his aggressive intentions and troop concentrations, have raised the tension in the area to a peak. Col. Nasser has created a position in which there is a danger of war.

On several occasions I have informed the Knesset and the nation of the growth in the power of the Israel Defense Forces. Today our army is at the zenith of its strength in manpower, skill, fighting spirit, and military equipment.

We must devote our attention not only to ensuring the freedom of passage, but also to the danger of military aggression led by Egypt. No sensible person will find it difficult to understand that so long as there exists a massive concentration of the forces of Egypt and her allies in the neighborhood of our borders, a conflagration could break out. The Israel Defense Forces will therefore remain mobilized, at arms, ready for any test, and if the necessity arises they have the strength to defeat the aggressors.

Egypt's measures constitute a threat to peace in the whole of our area. The Egyptian President's inflammatory declarations and threat implant illusions in the hearts of his excitable devotees. The Egyptian ruler should remember that this is not the first time that he has been borne on the wings of his imagination, seeing himself a victor before he has gone out to war. He should remember that his disappointment was not long delayed, as we ourselves have witnessed.

Mr. Speaker, Members of the Knesset:

The situation imposes on the country, on the whole nation and all the citizens, a heavy burden. We shall make every effort to ensure that the mobilization of the reserves shall not disturb the course of our economic life and the life of the individual more than is absolutely necessary.

In these days, we are witnessing wonderful and widespread manifestations of the voluntary spirit among all parts of the people. Out of the midst of our ordinary, everyday lives, powerful currents of devotion, responsibility, and loyalty break through to the surface. Israel is united in her understanding of the test that confronts her. Israel is faithful to herself, to her character, and to her ideals. These days will yet be remembered as a wonderful manifestation of national maturity.

I feel it my duty to say, from this rostrum, a few words to the Israel Defense Forces, to our soldiers, who stand ready at this hour in the expanses of the Negev, in Galilee, along all our borders, in the air and at sea. As in every one of the tests we have met since the rise of the State, so in these days the citizens of Israel and the world draw confidence and strength from that wonderful phenomenon, the Israel Defense Forces.

Planning, organization and execution, mass mobilization, the excellent armament, the determined deployment and the complete readiness for any mission—all these have been marked by superior skill, knowledge, and judgment, and accompanied by splendid manifestations of unbounded dedication.

You know, better than any, how much our strength has increased in recent years. The superiority of your forces to those of our enemies is today, more than ever, the guarantee of our security. By virtue of the power of your forces to defeat the enemy in any situation, the Government of Israel is capable of taking, with confidence and fortitude, the difficult decisions that confront it by virtue of our supreme responsibility for the fate of our country and the Jewish people.

We have complete confidence that, by maintaining your vigilant readiness, your strong morale, and your faith in the justice of our struggle, you will continue in the days to come to guarantee Israel's security and rights in the face of the challenges she confronts. In the name of the Government, the Knesset, and the entire nation, we thank you for all you have done so far and send you the greeting: be strong and of good courage to meet the future.

Mr. Speaker:

I cannot, of course, go into any greater detail in describing the situation. The members of the Foreign Affairs and Security Committee receive continual reports.

Members of the Knesset:

Confident in the Israel Defense Forces, encouraged by the growing support and sympathy we have received from other nations, fortified by the enthusiastic identification of the Jewish people with our cause, we stand on guard, ready to repulse any threat, any danger and any blow, until we attain security and peace.

Broadcast to the Nation

June 5, 1967

Citizens of Israel:

Since the hours of this morning our forces, on land and in the air, are returning war with a view to vanquishing the armies of the aggressive ruler of Egypt.

Egypt has forced a military campaign upon us, and all of us—the entire nation—the soldiers in the front line and the civilians in the rear, shall stand fast with courage and good cheer. We shall repulse the enemy and defeat his army.

Throughout the years since he assumed power, the ruler of Egypt has been announcing his plan and his preparations to attack Israel in order to destroy her. During the past three weeks he has not concealed from the world the fact that the time has come to carry out his scheme.

A great army, with its armor, cannons and planes, has been moved into east Sinai and posted close to our southern border; the UN Emergency Force has been ejected and the Strait of Tiran has been blocked to Israeli and to international shipping.

Arrogantly and braggingly, Nasser has made a

mockery of international law, has scorned the Charter of the United Nations, and has brought to nought mankind's aspiration to peace.

In addition to the agreement between him and Syria, the Egyptian ruler has, during the very days, concluded military treaties with Jordan and Iraq with the purpose of encircling us with an ever-tightening noose.

Our forces are strong enough to frustrate the schemes of the aggressor.

Israel strives for peace, but in order to protect peace we have built up mighty, resourceful, well-trained defense forces, equipped with top-quality modern weapons and deployed according to the best rules of military warfare.

Our soldiers—on land, in the air and at sea—are accompanied by the love and trust of the nation, are inspired by a spirit of bravery and are commanded by a capable and experienced corps of officers. Our army is deployed against any danger, capable of defending the State and defeating any aggressor.

The nation sends its blessings to its soldiers who dedicate their lives to the defense of our country: Be courageous and of good cheer!

To the citizens in the rear I say: Let each and every one of you manifest level-headedness; let everyone do his job, with dedication and efficiency, and put all his forces at the service of victory.

During these days which are liable to be a time of a cruel and bloody campaign, the distinction between front and rear may become blunted. In these days the entire nation is an army, all of Israel is a frontline. Each and every one of us, wherever he may be, and at all times, is in duty bound to consider himself responsible for the defense of Israel. All of us, headed by our army, shall vanquish those rising up against us.

Today we shall know who will lend us his support. These days are a testing time for the nations of the world—whether they will join in the heavy campaign, lend a loyal hand to our defense, and help us check the aggressor.

I fervently hope that peace-loving nations and states will not stand by but will understand the right of Israel to live its life without the sword of aggression hanging over its head.

At this juncture let us point to the ever-growing wonderful manifestations of solidarity on the part of Jews throughout the world. This solidarity of the Jewish people with the State of Israel elates us and inspires us with confidence. The feelings of brotherhood and unity which throb in the heart of every Jew brings far ones close and builds bridges across distances. The Jewish heart, wherever it is, now beats with the State of Israel, yearning for its victory.

Citizens of Israel!

Even as the cannons roar we shall not cease from longing for peace. Our only desire is to remove from our borders any threat of sabotage and every danger of aggression, to safeguard our security and the fullness of our rights.

Again we announce: We shall not attack any state as long as it does not wage war against us. But anyone attacking us will meet with our full power of self-defense and our capacity to defeat his forces.

Moreover, the Israel Defense Forces have been instructed to refrain from hitting the civilian population, but it is only proper for the enemy to know that these orders will remain in force only as long as *he* does not hit our population.

Today we stand up in the battle forced upon us, consolidated and strong as we have never been before, trusting in the Rock of Israel, relying upon the valor of the Israel Defense Forces and their power to defeat our enemies and to safeguard peace.

Address to the Chief Rabbis and Spiritual Leaders of All of Israel's Communities

June 7, 1967

HONORABLE CHIEF RABBIS, HONORABLE COMMUNITY LEADERS:

I have taken the liberty to call you to this meeting in order to enable you to share with me the news of the events taking place these last few days in Jerusalem, the Holy and Eternal City.

On the Monday of this week, after the Egyptian aggression against Israel began, I announced in a radio broadcast that Israel would take no military action against any state that did not attack her. Despite this statement, the Government of Jordan—under Egyptian command—declared war upon the State of Israel and its forces and embarked upon hostile action by land and in the air. Our forces were compelled to take the necessary military steps in order to put an end to this aggression and to protect human lives. By its actions, the Government of Jordan, with the agreement of Egypt and following upon pressure from Cairo, violated international law, the United Nations Charter, and the neighborly relations between our two countries.

In its aggression Jordan made no distinction between civilians and soldiers.

Crime was piled upon crime by Jordan when it carried war into Jerusalem, thus desecrating the eternal peace of this city, which has always been a source of hallowed inspiration to mankind. As a result of Jordanian aggression, dozens of people were killed and many hundreds were wounded. Blood was shed in the streets of Jerusalem and hundreds, perhaps thousands, of dwellings were hit. There was shelling specifically directed at hospitals, synagogues, Yeshivoth, the President's Residence, the Hebrew University, the Israel Museum and Government building. Likewise a large number of schools in the city were hit. The shelling continued uninterruptedly from Monday until today, Wednesday. Out of consideration for the sanctity of the city, and in accordance with our policy of avoiding casualties among the civilian population, we have abstained from any answering action inside the city, despite the casualties incurred by our soldiers and citizens.

The criminal actions of Jordan's government shall stand before the court of international opinion and before the judgment of history.

Peace has now returned with our forces in control of all the city and its environs. You may rest assured that no harm whatsoever shall come to the places sacred to all religions. I have requested the Minister of Religions to get in touch with the religious leaders in the Old City in order to ensure regular contact between them and our forces, so as to make certain that the former may continue their spiritual activities unhindered.

Following upon my request, the Minister of Religions has issued the following instructions:

a) arrangements in connection with the Western Wall shall be determined by the Chief Rabbis of Israel;
b) arrangements in connection with the Moslem Holy places shall be made by a council of Moslem clerics;
c) arrangements connected with the Christian Holy places shall be made by a council of Christian clergy;

With the aid of the Rock and Salvation of Israel, from Jerusalem, a symbol of peace for countless generations, from this Holy City now returned to its peace, I would like to have you join me in this call for peace among all the people of this area and of the whole world.

Statement in the Knesset

June 12, 1967

A WEEK AGO the momentous struggle opened. The existence of the State of Israel, the hope of the generations and the vision that has been realized in our days, hung in the balance.

Now, only a week after the last session of the Knesset, which took place to the accompaniment of the thunder of the guns, we meet with the tidings of victory ringing in our ears. The aggression of the enemy has been repulsed, the greater part of his power has been broken, his military machine destroyed, the bases for aggression cleared. The threat of war has been lifted from our country. The skies above our heads are safe. The threat to Jerusalem, to the coastal plain, to the villages of the north and the corridor, to the whole of the Negev and Galilee, has been removed.

The Israel Defense Forces dominate the Sinai Peninsula as far as the Suez Canal, the west bank of the Jordan, and the Golan Heights. The passage through the Strait of Tiran to the Gulf of Aqaba is free. Jerusalem has been re-united. For the first time since the establishment of the State, Jews pray at the Western Wall, the relic of our sacred temple and our historic past, at Rachel's Tomb. For the first time in our generation, Jews can pray at the Cave of Machepela in Hebron, the city of the patriarchs. The prophecy has been fulfilled: "There is recompense for the work, the sons have returned to their borders."

Now that victory has been won, let us bow our heads in reverent memory of the fallen. Hundreds of soldiers of the Israel Defense Forces and civilians have given their lives for this victory. I know that there can be no consolation for the loss of the individual and the bereavement of a family. Every living soul is an entire universe. Let all the bereaved families know that there can be no cause more just and vital than that for which the fallen fought. Let them know that by their deaths they bequeathed life to all of us. In the name of the entire nation, in the name of the Government and in my own, I assure them that we share in their grievous sorrow.

We shall always remember our dear sons, the soldiers of the Israel Defense Forces and their bold, valorous officers, whose place was always in the van, who have sanctified our people by their lives and their deaths. They join the long chain of heroism and self-sacrifice with those who have offered themselves up entirely on the altar of Israel and its land —a chain that will never be broken.

To the wounded we wish a speedy recovery and a return to active and useful life. No one who has seen the wounded in our hospitals can fail to be moved at their courage and fortitude. We are grateful from the bottom of our hearts to the doctors, nurses, and auxiliary staff, particularly to the volunteer physicians and others who have come from abroad to help in the sacred work of healing the sick.

These have been glorious and awesome days. Our people will remember them for generations to come. They were days when the spirit of man rose to new heights. The entire nation mobilized its strength to fight for its life and its hopes. Each individual felt that it was his responsibility to do the work, and he did his duty—every man at his post.

In the course of the years—confronting, as we did, the constant threats of our enemies—we were compelled to build up the defensive and deterrent power of the Israel Defense Forces, and devoted extensive resources to their training and equipment. The Israel Defense Forces constitute a mighty fighting force, as the whole world has learned, because of their high standards, because its officers and men are second to none—above all, because every man and officer is inspired by the mission of our people in its land. Our forces are a people's army: when they fight, the entire nation fights; when they fight, the whole of Jewish history watches them. When our army fights, it fights not only for the life of the people, but for its redemption.

Our people stood the test because it was united, because at the fateful hour it was able to concentrate its efforts and act as one man.

The people stood the test. Hundreds of thousands of young people and new immigrants, in big or little tasks, each according to his age and his abilities, proved that their roots in this country are eternal. It was shown that the spirit of the people flows from the spiritual revival of the State.

We saw clearly that this is no mere ingathering of exiles, but a new—yet ancient—nation, a united nation, which has been tempered in the furnace into one Israel, forged out of all our tribes and the remnants of scattered communities—they, their sons and their daughters. A nation has come into being which is ready for any effort or sacrifice in order to achieve its goals.

The State of Israel has stood the test because it knew that it carried the hopes of the entire Jewish people. The unity of our people has been forged anew in these days. All the Diaspora communities were keenly conscious of their solidarity with the State of Israel, the heart of the Jewish people. Thousands of our people came forward to help. Hundreds of thousands, millions, are ready to give us all the assistance in their power. Even those who are unable to offer their aid have their hearts with us in our struggle. Just as our own country has attained a higher unity, so has the unity of the Jewish people been reinforced. Jerusalem has been joined together, and in its unity, as our sages said, it has made all Israel brethren.

The last four weeks have been weeks of tension and trial—from Independence Day, the fifth of Iyar (May 15), until that great sabbath, the second of Sivan 5727 (June 10, 1967).

On Independence Day, powerful Egyptian forces started to cross the Canal and move in the direction of the Israeli frontier. After three days, these forces were deployed on our border.

Once the deployment was completed, Nasser demanded the withdrawal of the UN force from Sharm-a-Sheikh, Sinai, and the Gaza Strip.

On the morning of Tuesday, May 23, Egypt announced the closing of the Strait of Tiran to Israeli shipping and to international shipping carrying strategic material to Israel's southernmost port, Eilat.

After the Egyptian ruler had annulled the international arrangements that had been in force for the past ten years, he went on to proclaim in public his desire to wipe Israel off the map. As has now transpired, the commander of the Egyptian air force issued, on May 27, a secret operations order to his pilots to prepare for a surprise attack on Israel.

On May 30, Nasser signed a military agreement with Hussein. On June 4, he signed a similar agreement with Iraq. These agreements, in addition to the Egyptian-Syrian agreement, completed the encirclement of Israel—which was designed to facilitate a surprise attack upon us from all quarters.

On June 3, the then commander of the Egyptian forces in Sinai issued an order of the day to his soldiers to prepare for an attack on Israel, describing the expected results of "this unique moment" as "of historic importance to the Arab people." His prophecy came true in a manner of which he did not dream at the time.

As the Egyptian forces advanced into the Sinai Peninsula, I ordered, with the consent of the Government, the beginning of the mobilization of the

Israel Defense Forces' reserves. As the threat increased in gravity, mobilization was expanded and our preparedness intensified.

In my statement to the Knesset on May 29, I informed you that our forces were "ready and prepared to frustrate the enemy's designs in all sectors and on all our borders."

On the same occasion, I suggested that the Egyptian ruler might "remember that this is not the first time he has been borne on the wings of his imagination and seen himself a victor before he has set out to war." I added that "he ought to remember that disappointment was not long in coming, as we witnessed."

To the Israel Defense Forces I said: "Thanks to your being strong enough to overcome the enemy in any situation, the Government of Israel is able to adopt in confidence and fortitude the grave decisions that confront it, as is dictated by our supreme responsibility for the fate of the country and the Jewish people."

Last Monday, June 5, 1967, 7–8 Egyptian divisions, 2 of them armored, were deployed in front of our border in Sinai; 900 tanks were dispersed along the border—200 of them opposite Eilat, with the aim of cutting off the southern Negev; along Israel's eastern border stood 60,000 Jordanian soldiers and 300 tanks; the Jordanian army had been placed under Egyptian command, and Egyptian commando units, as well as Iraq forces, had entered its territory.

On our northern border with Syria, 50,000 Syrian

soldiers were ready for the assault, and the entire border was sown with guns and mortars, dug in, fortified, and protected by concrete and steel.

Some 600 Egyptian, Jordanian, Syrian and Iraqi planes were ready.

During the days preceding June 5, Egyptian air sorties took place over Israeli skies.

The decisive moment came. Facing the movement of Egyptian forces to the Israeli border, our forces went out to repulse the enemy's aggression, and air and armored battles developed.

In a radio broadcast a few hours later, I declared: "We shall not attack any state so long as it does not wage war against us. But anyone attacking us will meet with our full power of self-defense and our capacity to defeat his forces." Despite this unmistakable warning, the Jordanian forces, which were under Egyptian command, started attacks and bombardments all along the line—especially in Jerusalem, where much blood was spilt.

At the same time, the Syrians started attacking the villages in the north from their fortified positions in the Golan Mountains.

By Thursday, June 8, Israel's forces had defeated the enemy in Sinai, the Gaza Strip, the whole of Jerusalem and the whole of the west bank.

On this occasion, I should like to point out that, despite the bombardment of Jerusalem by the Jordanian forces, which caused loss of life, injury to many, and much damage to property, we refrained from any bombardment inside the city, out of consideration for the sanctity of Jerusalem and in accordance with our policy of avoiding injury to the civilian population.

Immediately after the liberation of the city, before I went to the Western Wall, I invited the heads of the Christian and Moslem communities and told them: "You may rest assured that no harm of any kind will be permitted to the religious Holy places. I have asked the Minister of Religious Affairs to contact the religious leaders of Jerusalem in order to ensure orderly contact between them and our forces, and enable them to continue unhindered with their religious activities. From Jerusalem—the age-old symbol of peace, from the Holy City to which its tranquility has been restored—I want to join with you in issuing a call to peace to all the nations of the area and to the world at large."

Arrangements were immediately made to ensure that the arrangements in places sacred to Christianity should be entrusted to Christian religious dignitaries, and in places sacred to Islam, to Moslem religious dignitaries.

In view of the continuation of heavy bombardment by the Syrians on our villages in the north, the constant danger to the lives of men, women and children, and the grievous damage that was being done to the villages, we were compelled to act in order to silence the Syrian posts on the Golan and Bashan Mountains.

On Saturday, June 10, the Syrian heights were in our hands and the bases for aggression, which had threatened the villages in the north, hailing down damage and destruction upon them for nineteen years for the purpose of turning them into heaps of rubble, had been liquidated.

During the fighting, our forces destroyed some 450 enemy planes, and hundreds of tanks. The enemies' forces were routed in battle. Many ran for their lives or were taken prisoner. This is the first time since the establishment of the State that the threat to our security has been removed at one and the same time in the Sinai Peninsula, the Gaza Strip, Jerusalem, the west bank and the northern border.

In these battles, the soldiers of the Israel Defense Forces fought, in their tens of thousands, with indescribable courage and heroism. They showed infinite devotion and comradely loyalty, resourcefulness and skill. Officers advanced at the head of their units and threw themselves upon strong fortifications. Many fell or were wounded leading their soldier comrades. Soldiers risked their lives to extricate their comrades and save them from death and captivity. It was by virtue of this dedication and fraternity of fighters that we won. Happy the people that has such an army.

From this rostrum I wish to congratulate the Members of the Government, the Minister of Defense, the Chief of Staff, the senior officers in the field and at headquarters, the commanders of corps and formations, and all the officers and men of the Israel Defense Forces on land, at sea and in the air. I am confident that the entire nation and all the forces will welcome my special greeting to the air force, and to its present and previous commanders.

Parallel with the developments in the security

arena, we were confronted with a struggle on the international political scene. During the first days of the crisis, from Independence Day until Thursday, May 18, the entry of the Egyptian forces into Sinai was described in various capitals as an act of demonstrative show.

Egypt's demand for the withdrawal of the international force was hastily fulfilled by the Secretary General of the United Nations, without the advisory committee of the UN force being asked to approve this step in advance or the matter being submitted for discussion at the UN Security Council.

With the removal of the UN force, the international struggle grew tenser. Nevertheless, no international institution took action to prevent the approaching aggression or to get rid of the concentration of Egyptian forces on Israel's border. It is possible that the impotence of the international organization encouraged Nasser to persevere in his aggressive path and to block the Strait of Tiran. Even after the blocking of the Strait, the Security Council did not call upon Egypt to annul the blockade, although several of its members described this act as illegal and dangerous.

When the Strait was blocked, the United States and Britain started political action for the purpose of safeguarding freedom of passage. Israel ascribed importance to this international action. We regarded it as useful that international opposition to one of the central manifestations of Egyptian aggression should be intensified.

However, it soon transpired that Nasser was not

content with closing the Strait of Tiran, and that this aim was the destruction of Israel. Thus, while the powers were seeking a solution to the problem of the Strait in accordance with international law, the fighting began.

During the three weeks that preceded the fighting, the eyes of the world were opened, perhaps for the first time, to the real nature of the Arab policy of hostility and the true aggressive intentions of the Egyptian ruler, against which we had warned the world for many years.

In my Knesset speech of May 29, I noted that we had been greatly encouraged by the growing support and sympathy we enjoyed throughout the world. During the days that followed, this support and sympathy became a powerful flood which encompassed states, governments and peoples, and testified how widely the vision of Israel's resurgence had become a part of the pattern of world culture in our generation. In the days that preceded the battles, the world's anxiety for Israel's survival became a mighty manifestation, which strengthened our position and will fortify us in the political struggle that lies ahead.

I have no intention in this place to refute lying propaganda, but, for the sake of historic truth, I want to repeat again, in the most categorical fashion, that when Israel fought for her life, her sons fought alone. In this war of defense we were not assisted by any military force of any country in any form whatsoever.

I must point out that throughout the period when

Egypt and her allies were preparing for war and during the fighting itself, there was one great power which not only did not denounce their aggressive policy, but even helped the aggressors by political means. On Saturday, June 10, 1967, the Soviet Union announced the rupture of diplomatic relations with Israel, and she was followed by Czechoslovakia and Bulgaria.

Perhaps there is not much practical advantage to be gained, but it is our international duty to ask the Soviet Union how she, as a member of the United Nations, reconciled her declared policy of solving international disputes by peaceful means with the bestowal of massive armaments and military equipment on states that have publicly declared their intention of using these armaments in order to destroy a sovereign state, and how her policy is compatible with open support for the aggressor during the fighting.

Perhaps the leaders of the Soviet Union will now realize that it is their duty to assist in the effort to establish true peace in the Middle East. In the last official contact between us, we expressed the hope that relations will yet be maintained between our countries on the basis of a more profound understanding of Israel's problems on the part of the Soviet Union.

Mr. Speaker, Members of the Knesset:

When the State of Israel was born, nineteen years ago, the Arab armies tried to strangle it at birth. When the State successfully resisted them, armistice agreements were signed. In these agreements it was expressly stated, in the clearest terms, that their purpose was to serve as a transitional stage on the road to peace. And indeed, that was the attitude which Israel adopted towards them.

However, in the course of the years we found that our neighbors regard these agreements as an expedient for gaining time in order to prepare for renewed aggression, with the aim of destroying Israel. The United Nations chose to ignore this attitude on the part of the Arabs. The UN Charter obligates member-states not to use force or the threat of force, and to solve disputes by peaceful means. Yet the United Nations refrained from condemning Arab hostility towards Israel. Thus, for nineteen years, this unique situation, unparalleled in international relations, persisted.

All the nations of the world, their leaders and their representatives heard the incitement of the Arab leaders and the rattling of the swords that were entrusted to them, but they were silent.

To the nations of the world I want to say: be under no illusion that the State of Israel is prepared to return to the situation that reigned up to a week ago. The State of Israel arose and continued to exist as a matter of right, and this nation has been compelled to fight and fight again for that right. Alone we fought for existence and our security: we are entitled to determine what are the true and vital interests of our country, and how they shall be secured. The position that existed up till now shall never again return. The land of Israel shall no longer be a no man's land, wide open to acts of sabotage and murder.

We have already explained to the nations of the

world that we look, not backward, but forward—to peace.

We shall faithfully observe the cease-fire, if it is observed by the other side.

Members of the Knesset:

A new situation has been created, which can serve as a starting-point in direct negotiations for a peace settlement with the Arab countries. The historic contribution which the people of the world, headed by the great powers, can make towards the establishment of peace in our area is clear and unmistakable. They must address their demands, not to Israel, which has sought peace since she came into being, but to the Arab states, which have turned the Middle East into a focus of tension and a hotbed of ceaseless hatred during the past two decades.

Justice, logic, and morality demand that, after those twenty years of impotence, the powers should have the courage to tell the Arab states that the United Nations Charter obligates them, just as it obligates every other member-state, to solve disputes by peaceful means.

Today our area is at the crossroads. In one direction lie peace and true cooperation, resting upon the sincere desires of the peoples in the area and their true interests. In the other direction lies the danger of continued hostility and hatred because of the absence of stable peace.

The international community is faced not only with a moral test, but also with a test of its political sagacity. The sooner the arms race in the area is ended, the sooner steps are taken to bring peace nearer in the Middle East, the greater, perhaps, will be the contribution to the relaxation of general international tension.

To the Arab peoples I want to say: we did not take up arms in any joyful spirit. We acted because we had no alternative if we wanted to defend our lives and our rights. Just as you have a right to your countries, so we have a right to ours. The roots of the Jewish people in this country go back to primeval days. Throughout the generations, Israel in dispersion maintained its spiritual and material links with this country, it was never severed from it even when it went into exile.

Similarly, this land has kept faith with us, it has not given itself to any stranger. This historic and spiritual right of ours has been confirmed by international law and forged on the anvil of reality. Today the entire world realizes that no force can uproot us from this land.

There is no parallel in the annals of the nations to this unique bond between our people and its land. Perhaps the fact that we have successfully survived the three wars that have been forced upon us will finally convince those who refuse to recognize this fundamental truth that our ties with this land are deeper than the sea, because without it our people cannot live.

In these days, when false hopes for the destruction of Israel have been shattered, perhaps the Arab leaders will think again, perhaps they will consider the extensive suffering and losses which they have caused to their peoples—and which we, too, regret.

Perhaps they will realize the valuable resources that have been squandered on weapons of war instead of being utilized for economic and social progress, perhaps they will ponder on the blessings that can flow to all the peoples of the area from sincere cooperation among them. Only through such cooperation will the Middle East take its rightful place in the total picture of world culture and human progress.

Mr. Speaker, Members of the Knesset:

When the emergency reached its climax, the Government was expanded and a Government of national unity established. I should like to state that the expanded Government, including the Cabinet Committee on Security Affairs, has stood, and continues to stand, the test of national leadership. I am confident that, in national unity, we shall meet the tests that lie in store for us, ready for the political struggle and always seeking peace.

May the coming days deepen still further that wonderful feeling of devotion, unity, and spiritual exaltation, the bond between future generations and the unity of the entire House of Israel.

Israel has emerged stronger than before from the test of fire and blood. Faithful to herself and looking with confidence to the future, with the aid of the Rock and Redeemer of Israel, this nation shall yet dwell in safety.

Public Statement

June 27, 1967

MY COUNTRY HAS just passed through a fateful struggle for its very existence. At this occasion, I should like to make a statement:

So long as our neighbors will persist in their policy of belligerence and will make plans for our destruction, we will not relinquish the areas that are now under our control and that we deem necessary for our security and self-defense. If, on the other hand, the Arab states will agree to discuss peace with us and will forego their war against us, there is no problem I hope that we will not be able to solve in direct negotiations, for the benefit of all parties concerned.

The prospects of direct negotiations are better today, I would say, than they have been at any time in the last twenty years, because the Arab states should be closer than ever to recognizing the need to face realities in the Middle East. They have tried war three times. The time has come for them to try out peace. During the last two decades it has become abundantly clear that the so-called armistice regime that existed from 1949 to 1967 is not conducive to peace and is not, therefore, in the best interests of the peoples of the region—Israelis or Arabs. Past experience has also shown that third-party mediation can be of little help. If the Arabs are ready for peace, there is no reason why they should not agree to talk with us about it. If they don't want peace, third-party mediation would only serve as a screen behind which the Arab states could pursue their policy of non-recognition of Israel and belligerency toward it. The establishment of peace between Israel and her Arab neighbors will, once and for all, put an end to the use of the refugees as pawns in the political game and is bound to create the conditions for the solution of many problems—including, of course, the refugee problem. I am certain that the international community, together with the countries of our region, including Israel, would then succeed in bringing about a just and truly humane settlement of the refugee question.

That Jews and Arabs are capable of living together in harmony and cooperation was amply demonstrated in the recent crisis when Israel's Arab inhabitants stood by Israel, as loyal citizens, both before and during the severe military test through which we passed. Many of them volunteered their services in various capacities and played their part in the national effort. Also, a number of Druse units actively and courageously participated in the fighting.

The same will for neighborly relations was the mainspring of the exemplary attitude of our officers and soldiers towards the prisoners-of-war who fell into their hands. Not only were all the regulations of the Geneva Convention fully observed, but there are many instances in which our men went out of their way to lighten the lot of these prisoners—their former enemies. On the occasion of my visit to our wounded at Hadassah Hospital in Jerusalem, I saw also wounded soldiers from the ranks of the Arab armies who had fallen into our hands. These wounded of the enemy armies received the same excellent medical treatment that is accorded our own wounded soldiers.

I am happy to note that life in the area captured by the Israel Defense Forces is returning to normal. Many regular peacetime services and facilities, interrupted by the war, are functioning once again, and steps are being taken to restore the remaining services, as well, to normal order. Most of the inhabitants in these areas are cooperating in this effort, and we all hope that the wounds of the past will quickly be healed.

Every effort was made, in the course of the fighting, to protect and preserve the places sacred to the various faiths—at times even at the cost of military expediency. Whoever visits the areas captured by our forces can see for himself that nearly all of the places of worship have remained untouched. We have made arrangements to assure free access to the Holy places to all who wish to worship there—members of all faiths, in those areas and throughout Israel.

The future of the Middle East now hinges on what the governments of the region are prepared to do to fashion that future in the best interests of their peoples.

There are today indications that at least part of the Arab leadership is aware of the futility of attempting to return to the untenable conditions that prevailed in this region for so many years. They—like we—would probably prefer to see a "new deal" for the peoples of the Middle East. To what extent they will be prepared to translate this awareness into concrete terms will, in large measure, depend on the willingness of other nations the world over to put the full weight of their influence behind direct negotiations between the parties. Such negotiations are the only hope of achieving a genuine and enduring peace in the Middle East.

Our hand is extended to peace to all who are ready for peace.

Address at the Opening of the Economic Conference

April 1, 1968

IT GIVES ME great pleasure to welcome you in the name of the Government of Israel and on my behalf at the opening of this important conference. Welcome to Jerusalem. Your participation in this gathering is an expression of your vital bond with the life of Israel.

We have gathered here to lay another layer in the building of the great partnership between Israel and world Jewry—that partnership which embraces all spheres of life, from the spiritual ties of mutual interdependence to full cooperation in strengthening and assuring the progress of Israel's economy.

The critical days that preceded the Six-Day War and the period of the war itself strengthened this sense of partnership between the Jewish State and the Jewish world. Our spirits were lifted and we all deeply appreciated that spontaneous outburst of profound Jewish solidarity.

We are proud of having had the privilege of helping to bring about that great experience in the history of our long-suffering people. Now we must transform this emotional upsurge into a rational determination to work together for Israel's consolidation and development.

The Six-Day War concluded a chapter in the life of the State of Israel and started a new chapter. It marked a watershed between past and future. It created a new challenge, new realities.

Our security position has been transformed. Despite our fervent desire and persistent efforts for peace with our neighbors and for cooperation in the development of the Middle East, their hostility forced upon us a long-drawn siege and three wars within the space of two decades.

Until the Six-Day War, our lives were dominated by a sense of encirclement. The enemy's armies were stationed within a few miles of our population centers. Jerusalem, our capital, was slashed in two by barbed-wire fences, and on the walls of the Holy City stood enemy soldiers sniping and killing.

The Six-Day War has liberated us from this danger. Although victory has not yet brought peace, it gave the people of Israel a sense of security. No longer do hundreds of thousands of enemy soldiers, equipped with the finest of modern weapons, stand in military readiness opposite our major centers. A strategic depth has been created. It has strengthened our sense of security and our capacity to defend Israel against any sudden attack by the Arab states.

Despite terrorist attacks and border incidents, despite the rearming of Arab countries by the Soviet Union, the people of Israel now enjoy a basic security unlike anything they have had since we achieved our independence. This confidence is in the hearts of Israel's people. Surely, you must feel it as you see the way we live and as you take part in our constructive work.

In today's situation, I cannot forget the historic associations perpetuated in the Bible, our Book of Books, in a style with which no one in our generation can possibly compete. It is written in the book of Nehemiah:

> "But it came to pass, that when Sanballat, and Tobiah and the Arabians, and the Ammonites, and the Ashodites, heard that the walls of Jerusalem were made up, and that the breaches began to be stopped, then they were wroth.
> "And conspired all of them together to come and fight together against Jerusalem and to hinder it.
> "Nevertheless we made our prayer unto God, and set a watch against them day and night, because of them.
> "And Judah said, the strength of the bearers of burdens is decayed and there is much rubbish; so that we are not able to build the wall . . .
> "And it came to pass from that time forth, that the half of my men wrought in the work, and the other half of them held both the spears, the shields, and the bows, and the habergeons.
> "Everyone with one of his hands wrought in the work, and with the other hand held a weapon.
> "For the builders, everyone had his sword girded by his side, and so builded."

These are the words of Nehemiah, the son of Hachaliah, who came up to this country from the court of the King of Persia, two thousand five hundred years ago, to rebuild the ruins of Jerusalem. We cannot read these words without being deeply moved. These words are as meaningful today as they were then. You need only go to the Old City, to the Western Wall, stand in the place where Nehemiah and his men stood so long ago, and you will hear the echo of the voice of the long history of our people. Then you will understand the call of the hour, to ourselves and to you.

My Friends:

Our political situation has also been transformed. Today it is clear that there is only one way out of the blind alley in which the problem of the Middle East has been blocked up for the past twenty years: the way of peace. Our demand for direct negotiations between the parties, and for peace treaties that will solve the problems of the area is becoming more and more understood.

There is a deepening consciousness that the wall of Arab hostility must be breached once and for all. Their policies must be founded on the simple and basic fact of life that Israel is here. Israel is here to stay. This they must recognize. Peace must be based on this inevitable conclusion.

I have no intention to say that the situation today is entirely satisfactory, and that there is no room for anxiety. We are still striving to achieve security, and at times this struggle costs us dearly. Our enemies still threaten us. It happens that a friend may turn his back on us.

We have endured three wars, and we have learned

from them. We shall give our support to any constructive initiative that will help the Middle East to advance towards peace, but we cannot agree to a return of perils to our very existence that prevailed until the fourth of June. We look towards peace and security.

My Friends:

There has also been a change in our relations with the Jewish world. The bond that unites us has been strengthened. We have realized how stable and profound it is and we shall build upon it. The task that history has imposed on us is a dual one: partnership in life and partnership in action.

By "partnership in life" I mean aliyah—pure and simple.

We must double the Jewish population of Israel by the end of the century. We hope that a large part of the added population will come from Western countries. There are tens of thousands in these countries who want to come and settle here. It is good for Israel and good for them.

Israel needs more people—the new situation confronts us with new challenges and new prospects. Many Jews need Israel, which gives them a feeling of full partnership in this great creative enterprise of the Jewish people, as well as opportunities for progress and development.

The character of this aliyah will be different from those that came to this country up till now. We shall have to adopt new ways of absorption. The immigrants from America need different social and economic conditions than those who came from Russia and Poland, Yemen and Morocco.

We have already started to make changes; the new reality and the new immigration will lead to many more. We shall offer the immigrant improved material conditions, as well as better channels for social integration.

To absorb this immigration, to develop Israel to its full potential as a modern industrial state, we need a further economic leap forward. Partnership with world Jewry will help us to give the newcomers their most important need—creative work.

The investment of knowledge and experience in Israel, of devotion, of daring, of contacts with possible markets, of money and machinery—there are the essentials of rapid development.

The entire history of our settlement in this country has taught us this: development brings aliyah, and aliyah brings development. We need new enterprises. We need the investors, managers, engineers, scientists, researchers, foremen, and workers who will man these enterprises.

As you know Israel is not very rich in raw materials, but the Jewish people can make up for that lack by using and applying our most important raw material—the Jewish spirit and brain. Jews have helped to develop many enterprises and—yes, many economies. Today they are called upon to help develop the economy of the Jewish State.

This is, in brief, our goal and our plan for the future. It is a challenge both to you and to ourselves. The funds that the Jews of the world have contributed to Israel, through the U.J.A. and other similar campaigns, and the loans they have made, have produced and will continue to produce wonderful achievements in our country—achievements of growth and immigrant-absorption unparalleled anywhere in the world.

Donations require a sense of enthusiasm and solidarity, quite apart from any economic considerations or calculation of profits. But direct investments and partnerships in business enterprises are a different story. Here questions of economic soundness, and the profit-and-loss account, influence decisions.

Our economic policies are designed to create suitable conditions for investments, that will offer fair profits—profits that will attract investors.

The first condition for both investments and immigration is a thriving economy. In times of crises, or even mild recessions, interest in investment lags. From this point of view, Israel's economic condition today is more favorable.

After a period of adjustment, we are again in a period of sharply rising economic activity. We can see it in production, in demand, in employment. Production and markets are growing. Unemployment has been considerably reduced. We are endeavoring to teach and train the unskilled for work in suitable trades, as we approach full employment. I need not explain to you why a period of expansion is the best time for investment.

New investments will absorb many newcomers with technical qualifications of almost all types.

The healthy expansion of the economy enables us also to absorb more professional men as well as all kinds of other workers.

A second condition is profitability. I said clearly at last August's meeting that we always regarded fair profits for employers as not only permissible, but desirable and necessary. Here, too, there have been important changes since the war. Not only the expansion in the local economy improves profitability but the adjustment of the Israeli Pound to the new rate of exchange of the pound sterling has increased our competitive position in European and American markets and made exports more profitable.

It is our clear intention to persevere in the policy to stabilize and preferably lower production costs. We shall strive to prevent inflation. Inflation discourages sound investment and weakens a nation's ability to compete in world markets. In this policy we enjoy the clear and open support of the Histadrut, which is showing a profound sense of concern over the fate of the economy and a full understanding of the need for its sound and sustained development. I am confident that the recent merger of the Labor parties will contribute to labor's full cooperation in this policy of self restraint, higher output, greater productivity and improvement in labor morale.

We expect the employers to play their part in this policy and do their share to make their enterprise more competitive, keep prices stable, cut production costs per unit, and thereby earn their fair profits. Their contribution to price stability and vigorous competition can be very great. Whatever is good for the economy and for the country is good for the employer and good for the worker.

A third condition is greater efficiency in the economy. In this area economic adjustment policies of 1966 and 1967 have considerable achievements to their credit. Many enterprises have put their house in order and attained greater efficiency in production —both management and labor. The results were not fully visible in 1967, since limited demand prevented enterprises from producing up to their full capacity, but that is changing fast. In the coming period they will be plainly apparent—especially as we continue in our efforts for efficiency. Under prosperity, it may be easier to enhance efficiency, since labor mobility can increase.

We shall continue with our policy of exposing local producers to competition from imports, so as to increase the economy's competitive capacity. During the past few months, furthermore, we have submitted to the Knesset labor laws which will make labor relations more efficient, for the benefit of the economy and both the employer and the worker. These laws, when passed by the legislature, will come immediately into operation.

I shall not describe in detail on this occasion the many attractive investment incentives we offer. My colleagues, the Minister of Finance, and of Commerce and Industry, will give you full information on this point.

Gentlemen:

Before I conclude these remarks, I should like to

touch on two or three topics which have already arisen during our discussions and will no doubt come up again.

First, the question of the Government and the economy. In a modern state, the Government and the economy are interconnected in a thousand ways. Their mutual dependence is almost complete. But the Government should not take the place of personal initiative of employers and management. The Government's task is to provide favorable general conditions so that worthwhile initiative may have chances to succeed, and I mean any and all worthwhile initiative: private or public, capitalist or collective, local or foreign, Jewish or non-Jewish. The Israeli economy is so much in need of initiative, now and in the future, that we cannot afford to close off any source. We shall give our full aid to any constructive initiative that may come from anywhere in Israel or abroad—and leave it to the entrepreneurs to succeed to the best of their ability.

I must repeat emphatically that, although this gathering is devoted to a dialogue between Israel and Jewish businessmen, the gates of Israel are open to anyone who has the initiative to invest and operate in Israel. Each will receive the same welcome and same assistance.

Another remark: We often hear complaints about bureaucracy and red tape—we heard them at the August meeting. Let me ask you to be perfectly frank and open: Is it only Israel that suffers from this plague? This, of course, is no consolation and no excuse, and you shall hear what has already been done and what will be done in the future to improve and simplify procedures.

Still, I would not advise this meeting to devote most of its attention to this subject. We welcome constructive criticism and new ideas, but not just what you call griping and excuses. We want to hear from you as to what should be done. But, after all, our main concern is that this gathering should also have *practical* results in production, marketing and exports—now and continuously.

We have set ourselves bold targets, as you will see in the proposed development plan prepared by the Economic Planning Authority and presented to you. In the course of the next four years, by 1971, we must increase our production by over 40 per cent and our exports by over 80 per cent. Annual investments will have to be 80 per cent higher and employment 20 per cent higher by 1971.

These are bold and ambitious objectives. We cannot achieve them alone. With you who are here with us today and with your many colleagues, together with the entire Jewish people, we shall be able to carry out the tasks that confront us.

I wish this conference practical and stimulating deliberations and substantial results. The State and the people await the fruit of your efforts. Great responsibility rests upon us. Together we shall meet it!

Christman, Henry M.

State Papers of Levi Eshkol